Bulletin OF THE NATIONAL ASSOCIATION OF WATCH AND CLOCK COLLECTORS, INC.

(ISSN 0027-8688)

Published six times yearly during the months of
FEBRUARY, APRIL, JUNE, AUGUST, OCTOBER, DECEMBER

Office of Publication, NAWCC Building, 514 Poplar St., Columbia, PA 17512

Manuscripts being offered for publication, all editorial correspondence, and reports for inclusion in Chapter Highlights should be sent to the Editorial Dept., P. O. Box 33, Columbia, PA 17512. Changes of address, membership applications, and dues payments should be sent to the NAWCC, Inc., P. O. Box 33, Columbia, PA 17512. Phone 717-684-8261.

Editor: TERENCE M. CASEY

Associate Editor: AMY J. SMITH

Editors Emeriti .... {
L. D. STALLCUP, 1943-1946 (Deceased)
PROF. W. I. MILHAM, 1946-1949 (Deceased)
ROBERT A. FRANKS, 1949-1953 (Deceased)
EARL T. STRICKLER, 1953-1974 (Deceased)
DR. DOUGLAS H. SHAFFER, 1974-1984

Membership $25.00 per year; Outside the U.S. $32.00 per year (U.S. Funds on U.S. Bank).
Additional membership within family — no publications — $10.00 per year.

Second Class Postage paid at Columbia, PA 17512
POSTMASTER: Send address changes to NAWCC, Inc., P. O. Box 33. Columbia, PA 17512
©1984 by the National Association of Watch and Clock Collectors, Inc.

Statements of opinion made by Authors of Papers read before or appearing in the publications of the Association are accepted as the author's own. The Association assumes no responsibility for the accuracy or correctness of any statements of its contributors or advertisers.

VOL. XXVI, No. 5   October 1984

D1302539

Time Out

In the August BULLETIN, we talked about sharing information with other members through the BULLETIN. Sharing is the adhesive that cements our Association together. Sharing at the Chapter and local levels is critical in order to maintain a healthy, helpful organization. Chapter Officers and volunteers take of their time to benefit us members, and we members thank them all very much.

Just as sharing within the organization is important, so is sharing with those outside the Association. Here at Headquarters we regularly receive calls of inquiry from non-members. Generally, the callers are unclear as to our exact functions, but know of our existence, and need a horological helping hand. After explaining what the Association is about and helping as best we can, more often than not, the caller decides to join our Association. It appears that sharing information about ourselves with non-members is normally enticement enough to change a non-member to a new member. New members bring with them new ideas, new interpretations, and new interests which, when shared, further the horological development of each one of us.

So thank you all for sharing. Keep it up, both within and without the Association so that we, individually and collectively, can continue to move forward horologically.

SIGHT IMPAIRED MEMBERS
interested in the
BULLETIN ON CASSETTE TAPES
contact NAWCC Headquarters.

Terry Casey

The President's Message

Included with the August issue of the BULLETIN was the State of the Association. This publication was mailed to each member so that reports from the Council, Committees, Officers, and the Administrator could be read. I believe each member should be involved with the affairs of the Association, and be aware of all NAWCC activities. I urge each one to read the State of the Association Supplement.

We have a tremendous amount of talent going to waste among our members. I am asking you to share your talent with *all* members through the BULLETIN. Our new BULLETIN Editor is in need of articles for our publication, and we are all anxious to read these articles. I am asking you to put your information on paper for publication, and mail to Editor Terry Casey. Many of you can share experiences on how and where you located a watch or clock and how you restored it. The Editorial and Research Committees will gladly assist you in developing your articles.

Several Chapters have indicated an interest in documenting every tower clock in their particular area. Recently there has been interest expressed in forming a tower clock Chapter. I, along with many others, would like to have all tower clocks documented, the information stored in the Headquarters computer, and thus made available for all members.

I urge each of you to attend the NAWCC sponsored Seminar in Hartford, CT, October 25-27, 1984. See your MART for details.

The fund drive for the NAWCC Museum and Research Center is slowly but steadily coming along. (Please note the letter from our Development Officer in this issue on page 601.) We need more Chapter and Regional support now. We have asked each Chapter President to appoint a fund drive Chairman to work with Chairman Dr. Warner D. Bundens and Deputy Chairman Doris Ravel. Send the name to Doris Ravel at P.O. Box 33, Columbia, PA 17512.

Many of our members are not aware that a Roster with the address of every NAWCC member (except those that have asked that their names be deleted) was published in 1983 and is available at a cost of $3.00 from NAWCC Headquarters. This is a valuable tool for contacting fellow members.

Again I urge each member to join a local Chapter and attend meetings. Have a good time collecting clocks and watches.

Sincerely,

Gene L. Bagwell

Gene L. Bagwell, President, NAWCC

GENE L. BAGWELL, ROUTE 4, BOX 475-A, FLORENCE, MS 39073

Miniature 30-Hr. Brass, Weight Movements, 1840-1880

by Snowden Taylor (NY)
Professor of Physics, Stevens Institute of Technology

INTRODUCTION

The author, d u r i n g his recent study of the Noble Jerome patent movement,[1] became familiar with several 30-hr. brass, weight movements (all but one apparently not "direct relatives" of the Noble Jerome movement), which appear to have been designed to fit smaller cases than those needed for the Noble Jerome type movements. Collecting data on these movements seemed a worthwhile task.

Eight basic movements have been identified, plus three sub-varieties, making a total of eleven. No doubt some have been missed. All but one of the movements described here have four-arbor trains, permitting fewer turns of the main wheels and hence a reduced weight drop. Typical cases are ogees, but other empire styles are not uncommon, and even a kitchen clock has been reported.

Not included in this study are the early movements of Silas Burnham Terry and Eli Terry, Jr. (very likely also designed by S. B. Terry) which have already been very capably described by McMillan.[2, 3] However, a sub-variety of one of these Silas B. Terry movements has emerged.[48] It (see Figure 1) is very similar to the movement illustrated as Figure 6 in the McMillan article specified in Reference 2. The tooth counts are identical to those reported by McMillan,[2] except that the #3 strike wheel has 42T instead of 40T. Also not included is the earliest Noble Jerome Patent movement #1.111,[1] which used a 39T center wheel, instead of the later standard 36T wheel, resulting in a short pendulum, and which is found in short empire cases. Likewise excluded is the Davies Patent Lever movement #20.1,[1] which, by means of a 50T escape wheel, as compared to the standard 42T, is sometimes made compatable with a miniature case. The latter two movements have been completely described in the Noble Jerome work.[1] "Miniature triple-decker" clocks and "miniature empire" clocks have been reported, but these are miniatures in the sense that the case styles were usually used with large 8-day clocks. The

Fig. 1 Movement by Silas B. Terry in clock by Silas B. Terry; private collection.

531

"miniature" cases are of "normal" size for the 30-hr. Noble Jerome type movements found in them, and are not included in this article.

It should be noted that occasionally the movements about to be described are found in standard sized cases. Also, as with the Noble Jerome movements, the miniatures were sometimes used with American (reverse) fusees, in order to accommodate them to cases designed for spring clocks.

The miniature movements will be described in the order in which the author estimates that they were developed, as they do not (except for the sub-varieties) appear to be related to each other.

TYPE 1.1 — JEROME'S

The author is not aware of any clock with a 1.1 movement that has been described in the literature. The author has one complete report of such a clock,[49] and a rumor of another.[33]

The movement is a three-arbor timepiece. The tooth counts for both the time train and the motion work are identical to the standard Noble Jerome Patent movement #1.112,[1] except for the escape wheel which has 48T instead of the usual 42T. See Tables I and II for tooth counts of the movement (and all other movements described in this article). All of the wheels (except the escape wheel) and the small movement parts have the appearance of Jerome wheels and parts such as those used in late #1.21[1] movements, which are believed to date to about 1842.[1] See Figures 2c and 2d. The center shaft of the 1.1 movement even has the L-shaped wire used to

Fig. 2a Clock by "Jerome's," containing type 1.1 movement probably by Chauncey Jerome, collection of Joyce B. Wahler.

Fig. 2b Label of clock of Figure 2a.

Fig. 2c Type 1.1 movement probably made by Chauncey Jerome, from clock of Figure 2a.

Fig. 2d Back of movement of Figure 2c.

trip the strike mechanism of a striking movement. See Figure 2e. The plates of the 1.1 movement appear to have been designed for it, and the cord barrel is considerably smaller in diameter than that in the usual striking movement. See Figure 2e. The small bevel case is shown in Figure 2a. It has some peculiar features, such as the nailed-on mouldings. Nevertheless, overall, it appears to be an American product contemporary with the movement. The dial is unpainted brass with black numbers. The label is shown in Figure 2b. The format is unusual. The address on the label is not a known clock store location.

Movement 1.1 appears to be a product of the Chauncey Jerome, Bristol factory, about 1842, using mostly standard parts. Miniaturization was accomplished by an escape wheel of higher count (and hence a shorter pendulum), small cord barrel, and a short weight.

TYPE 2.1 — CHAUNCEY JEROME

Clocks containing type 2.1 miniature movements have been illustrated previously,[4, 5] and the author has had reports of a few others,[6, 7, 8, 9, 49] and of two cases without the original movements.[10, 11]

Fig. 3a Type 2.1 movement made by Chauncey Jerome, from clock by Chauncey Jerome, collection of the American Clock and Watch Museum.

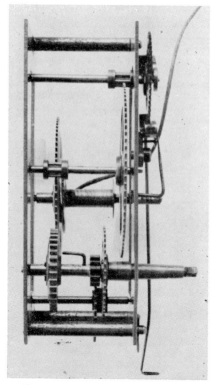

Fig. 2e Left side of movement of Figure 2c.

This movement has four arbors in both time and strike trains. Both #1 wheels are solid. The #2 strike wheel makes one-half revolution per strike, as compared to one revolution in the Noble Jerome standard design. The #2 arbor also carries two count wheel drive pins, two hammer lift pins, and the drop slot disc, which is sometimes solid and sometimes spoked. The strike train is arrested on warning by a pin on the #3 wheel. The back plate is made of sheet iron, without bushings. All aspects of the Noble Jerome patent are present, with only minor modification. The movement is shown in Figures 3a, 3b, and 4c. A case[7] is shown in Figure 4a. All known examples of the 2.1 movement have been found in such cases. The label[7] is shown in Figure 4b, and all known are the same, giving the location as Bristol, CT. The dials, which are not all identical, frequently have printed on them, "MADE BY C. JEROME, BRISTOL, CT. U.S.A." No New Haven label or dial

Fig. 3b Back of movement of Figure 3a.

has been seen. Two styles of the printed name have been observed. One form greatly follows the circular arcs of the dial.[4, 5, 6] The other does not[7] (see Figure 4a), and appears to have been intended for a larger dial, such as that of Reference 12, p. 152, which shows a wood movement clock of rather similar case style to that of the miniatures.

The author sees no strong reason to question that these movements were made by Chauncey Jerome in Bristol. The estimated date is 1843-44.

Fig. 4a Clock by Chauncey Jerome, containing type 2.1 movement by Chauncey Jerome, collection of Bryson Moore.

Fig. 4b Label of clock of Figure 4a.

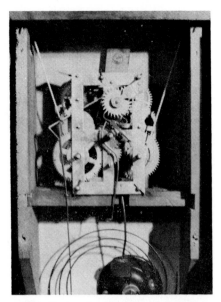

Fig. 4c Interior of clock of Figure 4a showing type 2.1 movement by Chauncey Jerome.

Fig. 5a Type 3.1 movement made by H. Welton, from "E. Terry's Cheap Thirty-Hour Clock," collection of the author.

TYPE 3.1 — H. WELTON

William L. Wadleigh, Jr., pioneered an interest in miniature 30-hr. brass weight clocks with his 1955 article, "Small Weight-Driven O.G. Clocks,"[13] in which he illustrated, among others, a clock with a 3.1 movement. Another early article,[5] undoubtedly by Brooks Palmer, illustrated the same clock. Roberts[14] discussed the possible origin of these clocks, and illustrated a label. The author has received a few reports of clocks with 3.1 movements[15, 16, 17, 33] and has commented on them in both the Noble Jerome work[1] and in his several-part article, "H. Welton & Co. — 1839-1846," which appeared in *The Timepiece Journal.*[18]

The mechanical features of the type 3.1 movement are essentially like those of 2.1: four-arbor trains, solid #1 wheels, one-half revolution of #2 strike wheel per strike, and a stop pin on the #3 strike wheel. All plates have pivot holes for an alarm mechanism, whether or not the alarm is used. The movement evades the Noble Jerome patent only through the use of a compound count wheel, consisting of a toothed wheel riveted to a slotted count wheel. (The patent calls for a one-piece toothed and slotted count wheel.[1]) See Figures 5a and 5b. All cases seen so far have been ogees. See

Fig. 5b Back of movement of Figure 5a.

Fig. 6 "E. Terry's Cheap Thirty-Hour Clock," containing type 3.1 movement by H. Welton, courtesy of George Beals.

Figure 6. The labels are the same in all observed clocks, and have a curious wording: "E. TERRY'S / CHEAP THIRTY HOUR / CLOCK, / MOVE-MENT MADE BY / H. WELTON, / TERRYVILLE, CONN. / The cost of this clock is but little more than one of the common Clocks, which are so plentifully manufactured / at the present time, and is a much better article, and as cheap a Clock as any man would buy for his own use, /

provided, he understood Clockwork, and knew what he was buying. / DI-RECTIONS . . . / . . . / PRESS OF ELIHU GEER, . . . STATE STREET, HARTFORD." See Figure 6. Note that the wording on the label fails to mention the maker of the *clock*.

Fig. 7a "E. Terry's Cheap Thirty-Hour Clock," containing type 3.2 movement by H. Welton.

Fig. 7b Label of clock of Figure 7a.

Fig. 7c Type 3.2 movement with alarm, made by H. Welton, from clock of Figure 7a.

Fig. 8a "E. Terry's Improved Thirty-Hour Clock," containing type 3.3 movement by Hiram Welton.

TYPE 3.2 — H. WELTON

The 3.2 movement has not been previously mentioned in the literature. It is identical to the 3.1 movement, except that the count wheel is a single wheel, toothed and slotted, and hence the 3.2 movement violates the Noble Jerome patent in all respects. Only one example has been observed, in an ogee case, with a label identical to that used with 3.1 movements.[19] See Figures 7a, 7b, and 7c. Note the alarm.

Fig. 8b Label of clock of Figure 8a.

Fig. 8c Back of type 3.3 movement made by Hiram Welton, from clock of Figure 8a.

TYPE 3.3 — HIRAM WELTON

The earliest reference, known to the author, to a clock with a 3.3 movement was in a 1955 Answer Box item [20] and a following response.[21] Wadleigh's article also included a clock with this movement,[13] and the same clock was shown in two other articles, undoubtedly by Brooks Palmer.[5, 22] Roberts[23] and Shaffer[24] each showed a clock with this movement. The author has received several reports on 3.3 movements,[19, 25, 26, 27, 28] one on an empty case,[29] and has mentioned them in two previous articles.[1, 18]

The 3.3 movement is a redesigned version of the 3.1 and 3.2 movements. The count wheel of 3.2 is retained, so 3.3 is in full violation of the Noble Jerome patent. The mechanism of 3.3 is identical to the earlier versions. However, the #1 wheels are spoked, the strike hammer arbor has been moved

Fig. 9a Case of clock by "H. Welton, Agent," containing type 3.3 movement by Hiram Welton, collection of Jacque Houser.

<————

Fig. 9b Label of case of Figure 9a.

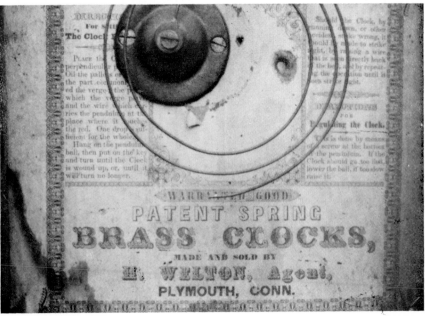

Fig. 9c Type 3.3 movement made by Hiram Welton, from case of Figure 9a.

slightly to the right, the position of the verge retainer wire has been changed, and a small heart-shaped opening has been introduced in the front plate behind the position of the verge pin. See Figures 8c, 9c, 9d, and 11c. All plates are drilled for alarms, and alarms are fairly common.

The 3.3 movements, when used with weights, are most commonly found in ogee cases (see Figure 8a), but sometimes in other small empire cases. The 3.3 movements were apparently sold on the market, and more often than not are seen in the clocks of users rather than makers. The maker's label seen occasionally in the weight clocks[19, 27, 29] is as follows: "E. TERRY'S / IMPROVED THIRTY HOUR / CLOCK, / MOVEMENT MADE BY / HIRAM WELTON, / TERRYVILLE, CONN." These words are followed by the same sentence regarding the quality of the clock that was quoted under 3.1 above. See Figure 8b. The 3.3 movements are found, fairly frequently, driven by reverse fusees, housed in steeple cases.[20, 21, 23, 24, 27, 28] See Figures 9a-9d. A rare maker's label occasionally seen on the

Fig. 9d Back of movement of Figure 9c.

Fig. 10 Interior of clock by Pettibone & Peters, containing type 3.3 movement by Hiram Welton, collection of Gene Georgetta.

Fig. 11a Clock by Silas B. Terry, containing type 3.3 movement by Hiram Welton, collection of Richard Baldwin.

Fig. 11b Interior of clock of Figure 11a.

Fig. 11c Type 3.3 movement made by Hiram Welton, from clock of Figure 11a.

fusee clocks[27, 28] states, "WARRANTED GOOD / PATENT SPRING / BRASS CLOCKS, / MADE AND SOLD BY / H. WELTON, Agent / PLYMOUTH, CONN." See Figure 9b. Users' labels seen in clocks with 3.3 movements are F. C. Andrews,[19, 26] Brewster & Ingrahams,[20, 21, 23] W. N. Johnson & Co.,[5, 13, 19, 22] Pettibone & Peters[25] (see Figure 10), Sperry & Shaw,[24] and Silas B. Terry[27] (see Figures 11a, 11b, and 11c).

TYPE 4.1 — HIRAM WELTON

Wadleigh's article[13] showed a clock with a 4.1 movement, and three subsequent articles,[5] almost certainly by Brooks Palmer, showed the same clock. Later articles by McMillan[30] and by Wood and Kramer[31] presented exam-

Fig. 12a "S. B. Terry's Alarm Timepiece," containing type **4.1** movement by Hiram Welton, collection of Richard Baldwin.

< ———

ples of clocks with this movement. Distin and Bishop[32] showed an example mounted "upside down" compared to the others. The author has received two reports on clocks with 4.1 movements.[27, 33]

Movement 4.1 is a timepiece. All but one of those reported are weight-driven alarm timepieces. The "upside-down" example shown by Distin & Bishop has no alarm, and is driven by a reverse fusee. Movement 4.1 has, again, a four-arbor train. When used as an alarm timepiece, the alarm is at the top of the movement. Below the alarm is the motion work; then the great wheel, with the time train running *down* from it. The escape wheel and verge are between the plates near the lower edge of the movement. See Figures 12c, 14c, and 14d.

Observed 4.1 movements have been in bevel[27, 30] (see Figure 12a) and miniature ogee[5, 13, 31, 32, 33] (see Figures 13a and 14a) cases. Maker's labels[27, 30, 33] read, "S. B. TERRY'S /

Fig. 12b Label of timepiece of Figure 12a.

ALARM TIMEPIECE: / MOVE-
MENT / MADE BY / HIRAM WEL-
TON. / ... / ... / PRESS OF ELIHU
GEER, STATE STREET, HART-
FORD." See Figure 12b. One clock[33]
has the maker's label covered by the
label of the user, J. J. Beals & Co. See
Figure 13b. Two other clocks[5, 13, 31]
have labels of user Daniel Pratt, Jr.
See Figure 14b. One article[5] reported
a 4.1 movement stamped "S. B. Terry

Fig. 13a Alarm timepiece by J. J.
Beals & Co., containing type 4.1 move-
ment by Hiram Welton, collection of H.
Bryan Rogers. (J. J. Beals & Co. label
overpasted on "S. B. Terry's Alarm
Timepiece" label.)

Patent" in a case with J. J. Beals
label. However, the author doubts this
report, and suspects the J. J. Beals
label is overpasted on the maker's
label, as in the clock described above.[33]

DISCUSSION OF THE
HIRAM WELTON MOVEMENTS

The author has studied the extant
account books of H. Welton & Co.,
1839-1846.[18] The company was a partnership between brothers Heman (the
businessman) and Hiram (the clockmaker). In the company name, "H."
stands for Heman and the "& Co." is
Hiram. The firm went bankrupt about
August 1, 1845, and the affairs of the
company were settled in 1846. The
author believes that whenever "H.
Welton" alone appears on a clock
label, this refers to Hiram Welton, the
clockmaker.

Fig. 12c Type 4.1 alarm movement
made by Hiram Welton, from timepiece
of Figure 12a.

Fig. 13b Label of
timepiece of Figure 13a.

Roberts[14] reported undocumented evidence that Eli Terry had designed a new movement for the Weltons in order to avoid infringing the Noble Jerome patent. Furthermore, Roberts speculated that the 3.1 movement was the one in question, since Eli Terry was named on the label. The author has discussed this possibility both in the Noble Jerome article[1] and the Welton article,[18] but has doubted this purpose, since movement 3.1 barely avoids the patent, and 3.2 and 3.3 do not avoid the patent at all.

An examination of the label quoted above for the 3.1 and 3.2 movement clocks, the first label quoted for the 3.3 movement clocks, and the label quoted for the 4.1 movement timepieces, reveals a common peculiarity: none of them state the maker of the *clock*. The author has suggested[1, 18] that this might be a clue to a clock produced during a bankruptcy. The Welton ac-

counts[18] show clearly that production of clocks continued during bankruptcy, as was common practice. In early 1846, just before the end of the H. Welton & Co. account books, a new firm seems to have been formed: "James Beach (Hiram Welton, Agt.)." This firm appears to have purchased parts, small tools, and supplies from the bankrupt company, and appears to have rented larger furnishings and machines.[18] One assumes that Hiram Welton, in the midst of a bankruptcy, could not do business under his own name. The author speculated[1, 18] that the firm James Beach (Hiram Welton, Agt.) was the maker of the movements under discussion. Now there have come to light the clocks with the label "H. WELTON, Agent," the second label quoted under 3.3 above. See Figures 9a-9d. These clocks provide strong evidence in confirmation of the author's speculations.

543

Fig. 14a Alarm timepiece by Daniel Pratt, Jr., containing type 4.1 movement by Hiram Welton, collection of NAWCC Museum.

<———

Supporting evidence for this conclusion is as follows: Hiram Welton had been movement maker for Eli Terry, Jr.[34] Terry's father, Eli, Sr., had continued to experiment with clocks after retirement, and Silas B. Terry appears to have operated the "experimental shop" for the family.[14] All had close ties together. The solid #1 wheels of the 3.1 and 3.2 movements are suggestive of Silas B. Terry. Note, above, that a 3.3 movement has been seen in a Silas B. Terry case.[27] A Silas B. Terry movement of the Noble Jerome type (#2.5)[1] has been found in an ogee clock with the label of M. Welton, New York. Merit Welton was a cousin of Hiram and Heman,[35] and his New York store was sometimes used as a sales outlet for H. Welton & Co. clocks.[18]

Fig. 14b Label of timepiece of Figure 14a.

Fig. 14c Back of type 4.1 alarm movement made by Hiram Welton, from timepiece of Figure 14a. ————————>

Fig. 14d Perspective view of movement of Figure 14c.

TYPE 5.1 — ELISHA MANROSS

A Vox Temporis letter in 1959 re_
ferred to a clock with a 5.1 movement
and briefly described its operation.[36]
The author has received reports of
three others.[17, 37, 38]

This movement, again, has four arbor trains, time and strike. The #2
strike wheel turns one-fifth turn per
hammer strike, rather than the one
turn of the Noble Jerome standard design. The count wheel is centrally located on a stud on the inside of the
back plate of the movement, and is
driven by five pins on the #2 strike
arbor. Five driving pins can also be
viewed as a five-leaved open-ended

Fig. 15b Label of clock of Figure 15a.

Fig. 15a Clock by Elisha Manross, containing type 5.1 movement by Elisha Manross, collection of the author.

Fig. 15c Type 5.1 movement made by Elisha Manross, from clock of Figure 15a.

Fig. 16a Clock by George Brown, containing type 5.1 movement by Elisha Manross, collection of NAWCC Museum.

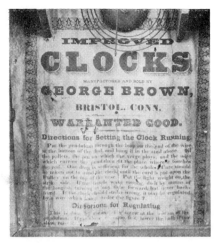

Fig. 16b Label of clock of Figure 16a.

Fig. 16c Back of type 5.1 movement made by Elisha Manross, from clock of Figure 16a. (Metal plate behind strike side winding drum is a repair.)

Fig. 16d Perspective view of movement of Figure 16c.

Fig. 17a Clock by Elisha Manross, containing spring-driven movement by Elisha Manross similar to type 5.1, collection of the author. (Tablet may not be original to this clock.)

lantern pinion. The #2 strike wheel has five hammer lift pins. The lift wire on the same arbor as the count hook is extended to play against the same five hammer lift pins, which then lift the count hook clear of the teeth of the count wheel. At the end of striking the hour, the train is arrested by a pin on the #3 strike wheel, and this pin also arrests the train at warning. Since lifting the count hook and stopping the strike are the two functions of the drop slot disc in the standard Noble Jerome design, no drop slot disc is needed in the 5.1 movement, and the movement thus evades the Noble Jerome patent. (The 5.1 arrangement is similar to that used on the 30-hr., spring, cast iron backplate movement of E. C. Brewster.[39]) Both #1 wheels have wooden cord barrels, which appear to be pressed onto the steel arbors. See Figures 15c, 16c, and 16d. Without these wooden barrels, and with a 42T escape wheel instead of 39T, the 5.1 movement would be a standard Manross 30-hr. spring movement.[17] See Figures 17a-17c. Hence the weight movement is believed to have been developed from the spring movement.

All 5.1 movements observed to date have been housed in ogee cases, some miniature[17, 38] (see Figure 15a) and one standard[37] (see Figure 16a). Some movements are on seat boards like regular weight clocks,[36] and some are attached to the back of the case with wooden clips, as in spring clocks.[17, 37] An Elisha Manross label in one clock[17] is shown in Figure 15b. This label bears the imprint "PRESS OF ELIHU GEER, 10 STATE STREET, HARTFORD." Roberts[23] places Geer at this address 1850-1856. Users' labels have been seen for Terhune & Botsford[36] and George Brown.[37, 38] See Figure 16b. The 5.1 movements are clearly Elisha Manross products, probably dating to the early 1850's.

Fig. 17c Spring movement by Elisha Manross similar to type 5.1, from clock of Figure 17a.

TYPE 6.1 — HENRY TERRY / SILAS B. TERRY

Clocks with 6.1 movements were illustrated in an early article, undoubtedly by Brooks Palmer,[5] and by Dworetsky & Dickstein.[12] Clocks which probably contain this movement were shown by Palmer,[4] by Distin & Bishop,[32] and in an auction catalog.[40] The au-

Fig. 17b Label of clock of Figure 17a.

548

Fig. 18a Clock by Henry Terry, containing type 6.1 movement by Silas B. Terry.

Fig. 18d Back of movement of Figure 18c.

thor has received four other reports[19, 41, 42, 48] on clocks with 6.1 movements, and one report[11] on a movement in an incorrect case.

The 6.1 movement has four-arbor

Fig. 18c Type 6.1 movement made by Silas B. Terry, from clock of Figure 18a.

trains and solid #1 wheels. The count wheel, concentric with the #2 strike arbor, is driven by a 14T gear on the #1 strike arbor, thus avoiding the Noble Jerome patent. The gearing works out to one-third turn of the #2 strike wheel per strike, and the #2 strike arbor carries three hammer lift pins and a disc with three drop slots. The #3 strike wheel carries the warning stop pin. See Figures 18c and 18d.

Movement 6.1 is usually found in miniature ogee c a s e s[4, 5, 12, 19, 32, 40] (see Figure 18a), but sometimes in other miniature empire cases.[42] These clocks are most commonly found with what appears to be maker's labels of Henry Terry,[4, 5, 12, 19, 32, 40] with printer's line "PRESS OF ELIHU GEER, 10 STATE STREET, HARTFORD." (See Figure 18b.) A few have a user's label of William S. Johnson.[19, 42] Roberts[23] gives Geer at the above address 1850-1856. It is almost certain that Henry Terry was not actively involved in the clock business at that date.[14] The 6.1 movement shows considerable similarity to a spring movement made by Silas B. Terry. See Reference 43, for example. Bailey, in his history of S. B. Terry,[44] points out that Henry Terry helped his brother Silas financially on a number of occasions. Bailey attributes clocks such as those with 6.1 movements and Henry Terry labels to some such occasion, perhaps in 1855.

Fig. 18b Label of clock of Figure 18a.

Fig. 19a Clock by The Terry Clock Co., containing type 7.1 movement by The Terry Clock Co.

It would appear that, with some confidence, one can attribute the 6.1 movement to Silas B. Terry some time in the first half of the 1850's.

An early article,[5] almost certainly by Palmer, showed a Wm. S. Johnson miniature ogee clock with a "second hand" which turned 1½ revolutions in a minute. This could be a 6.1 movement clock, since a hand placed on the escape arbor would turn at just that rate. Distin & Bishop[32] illustrated a miniature ogee clock by S. B. Terry & Co. (1852-53[44]). This clock could contain a 6.1 movement.

TYPE 7.1 — THE TERRY CLOCK CO.

The author has received one report[19] on a clock with a 7.1 movement.

The 7.1 movement again has four-arbor trains. The m o v e m e n t is stamped, "THE TERRY CLOCK CO. / WATERBURY CONN. / PAT'D DEC 1, 1868," but virtually no elements of the patent[44] are incorporated.[50] Both #1 wheels are solid. The count wheel is mounted on a stud on the back of the back plate and is driven by three pins on the #2 strike arbor. This arbor turns one-third revolution per strike, and carries the drop slot disc with three drop slots and three hammer lift pins. Hence all elements of the Noble Jerome patent are present. The #3 strike arbor carries the warning stop pin. The escape wheel is between the plates. See Figures 19c and 19d.

The movement is housed in an ogee case.[19] See Figure 19a. The label is shown in Figure 19b. It is inscribed "American Printing Company, Waterbury, Conn." Clearly this movement was made by The Terry Clock Co. Dating is more uncertain. The company went bankrupt in 1880. Hence 1868-1880 is a safe date range. In light of movement 7.2 (see below), one can probably guess that the 7.1 movement dated to the earlier part of this date range. H. Bryan Rogers has prepared an excellent paper in which the 7.1 and 7.2 movements are discussed in more detail.[50]

Fig. 19c Type 7.1 movement made by The Terry Clock Co., from clock of Figure 19a.

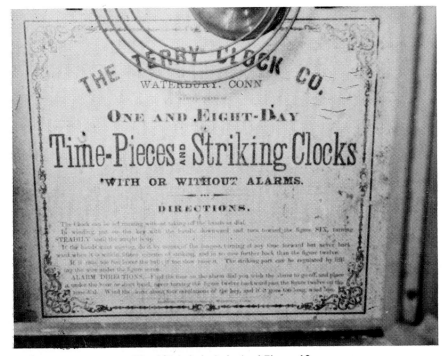

Fig. 19b Label of clock of Figure 19a.

551

Fig. 19d Back of movement of Figure 19c.

Fig. 20b Label of clock of Figure 20a.

TYPE 7.2 — THE TERRY CLOCK CO.

The author has received two reports[33, 45] on clocks with 7.2 movements.

Movement 7.2 is a remodeled version of 7.1. It is mechanically identical to 7.1, but the #1 wheels are spoked and the escape wheel and verge have been moved to the front of the front plate. The latter has been accomplished by sawing out most of the upper vertical bar of the front plate.[50] There have also been some changes in the spoking of various wheels. See Figures 20c and 20d. Movement 7.2 is stamped either like 7.1[45] or, "TERRY CLOCK CO. / PAT'D DEC. 1, 1868."[50] The latter is believed to be the later stamp. Movement 7.2 contains no vestige of the patent elements.[50]

Fig. 20a Clock by The Terry Clock Co., containing type 7.2 movement by The Terry Clock Co., collection of H. Bryan Rogers.

Fig. 20c Type 7.2 movement made by The Terry Clock Co., from clock of Figure 20a. ————>

552

Fig. 20d Back of movement of Figure 20c.

The 7.2 movements observed have been in miniature column and cornice cases.[33, 45] See Figure 20a. The labels are the same as in the clock containing the 7.1 movement, but at least one[33] is from a different printing. See Figure 20b. It is probable that the "One Day O.G. & O.O.G. Weight Strike" and "One Day Rose Column (Weight)" clocks of the 1875 catalog of The Terry Clock Co.[44] contained 7.2 (or perhaps 7.1) movements. These 7.2 movements are obviously products of The Terry Clock Co., and were made 1868-1880, probably not in the earliest part.

Fig. 21a Clock by New Haven Clock Co., containing type 8.1 movement by New Haven Clock Co.

TYPE 8.1 — NEW HAVEN CLOCK CO.

Six reports have been received on clocks with type 8.1 movements.[11, 16, 19, 38, 46, 47]

Again, type 8.1 is a movement with

Fig. 21b Label of clock of Figure 21a.

Fig. 21c Type 8.1 movement made by New Haven Clock Co., from clock of Figure 21a.

Fig. 21d Back of movement of Figure 21c.

four-arbor trains. Mechanically, the movement is similar to the type 2.1 movement: count wheel concentric with #1 strike arbor, driven by two pins on the #2 strike arbor which makes one-half revolution per strike, two drop slots and two hammer lift pins on the #2 strike arbor, and a warning pin on the #3 strike wheel. All elements of the Noble Jerome patent are present. See Figures 21c and 21d. One clock reported[19] has an outboard alarm.

All case styles reported, except one, have been miniature ogees.[11, 16, 19, 38, 46] Some of these,[19] such as that in Figure 21a, have been "usual" style ogees. At least one[16] was an ogee embellished in the V i c t o r i a n mode: round dial with surrounding brass ring supported on a thin wooden board, no cross-bar in the door, and blue-stained case interior to show off a decorative pendulum — all in the style of a "gingerbread" clock. Some of the others had one or more of these features.[11, 19] Labels in the ogees,[19] when present, are like that of Figure 21b. The one non-ogee was, in fact, a sort of gingerbread clock (called "Ganges" on the label).[47] See Figures 22a and 22b. The author suspects that the 8.1 movement is an adaptation of a spring movement, but has not been able to make a specific match. The estimated date range is 1875-1900.

Fig. 22a Clock by New Haven Clock Co., containing type 8.1 movement by New Haven Clock Co., collection of Joe Bartels. (Dial not original; alarm hub and alarm missing.)

CONCLUSIONS

In the eight basic movements plus three sub-varieties discussed in this article, all except 1.1 have a funda-

Fig. 22b Interior of clock of Figure 22a.

mental similarity, namely reducing the weight fall by increasing the number of arbors in the trains to four. Each accomplishes the result using different details. Except for the sub-varieties, none of the movements appear to have been copied from each other. Silas B. Terry seems to have had a hand in three or four of the eight basic types.

There are doubtless others of these miniature weight movements, and the author would be pleased to receive any reports of such. An early article, undoubtedly by Brooks Palmer,[22] illustrated one, a timepiece with a ladder movement. This movement may be a weight driven version of the movement shown in Palmer's TAC[4], p. 155, by S. B. Terry & Co. However, no further data are available.

ACKNOWLEDGEMENTS

The author wishes particularly to thank Richard Vallee, Chis Bailey of the American Clock and Watch Museum, Richard Baldwin, Paul Heffner, H. Byran Rogers, and Stacy Wood of the NAWCC Museum, as well as his sons, David Taylor and Rolf Taylor. The author also thanks Adolph Amend, Dick Babel, George Beals, Frank Boyce, Willard Fox, Ward Francillon, Gene Georgetta, Bob Higgins, Jacque Houser, Amerst E. Huson, Samuel Jennings, Lindy Larson, Bryson Moore, John Rawlings, W. L. Wadleigh, Jr., and Joyce B. Wahler. The Research Committee of NAWCC has sponsored some of the photographic work.

REFERENCES

1. Snowden Taylor, *The Noble Jerome Patent 30-Hour Brass Weight Movement and Related Movements,* The Westchester Chapter #90 and The Central New York Chapter #55, NAWCC, 1981; also, NAWCC BULLETIN, XXIV, 693 (1982). (Movement type numbers, when used in the present article, refer to the later article above.)
2. F. H. McMillan, NAWCC BULLETIN, XI, 914 (1965).
3. F. H. McMillan, NAWCC BULLETIN, XII, 26 (1965).
4. Brooks Palmer, *A Treasury of American Clocks,* The Macmillan Company, New York, 1967. The dimensions given for the clock with 2.1 movement are believed to be in error.
5. Don Maust, Ed., *Early American Clocks,* E. G. Warman Publishing Co., Uniontown, PA, 1971 (original articles almost certainly by Brooks Palmer).
6. Richard Babel, private communication.
7. Bryson Moore, private communication.
8. Collection of the American Clock and Watch Museum, Inc., Bristol, CT.
9. Frank Boyce, private communication.
10. John Rawlings, private communication.
11. Samuel Jennings, private communication.
12. Lester Dworetsky and Robert Dickstein, *Horology Americana,* Horology Americana, Inc., Roslyn Heights, NY, 1972.
13. W. L. Wadleigh, Jr., NAWCC BULLETIN, VII, 30 (1955).
14. Kenneth D. Roberts, *Eli Terry and the Connecticut Shelf Clock,* Ken Roberts Publishing Co., Bristol, CT, 1973.

15. A. E. Huson, private communication.

16. George Beals, private communication.

17. Collection of the author and family.

18. Snowden T a y l o r , Timepiece Journal *2*, 111 (1981) ; *2*, 123 (1982) ; *2*, 153 (1982) ; *2*, 171 (1983) ; and *3*, 12 (1983).

19. Richard Vallee, private communication.

20. W. F. P. in "The Answer Box," NAWCC BULLETIN, VI, 460 (1955).

21. E. P. H., K. D. R., and W. B. D., "The Answer Box," NAWCC BULLETIN, VI, 521 (1955). (K. D. R., who must be Kenneth D. Roberts, gave the right answer.)

22. Don Maust, Ed., *Early American Clocks, Vol. III*, E. G. Warman Publishing Co., Uniontown, PA, 1975 (original articles almost certainly by Brooks Palmer).

23. Kenneth D. Roberts, *The Contributions of Joseph Ives to Connecticut Clock Technology 1 8 1 0 - 1 8 6 2* , American Clock and Watch Museum, Inc., Bristol, CT, 1970.

24. D. H. Shaffer, NAWCC BULLETIN, Supplement 9 (1973).

25. Gene Georgetta, private communication.

26. Willard Fox, private communication.

27. Richard Baldwin, private communication.

28. Jacque Houser, private communication.

29. Bob H i g g i n s , Cog Counter's Journal No. 14, 14 (1977).

30. F. H. McMillan, NAWCC BULLETIN, XI, 484 (1964).

31. Stacy B. C. Wood, Jr., and S. E. Kramer III, NAWCC BULLETIN, XX, 160 (1978).

32. William H. Distin and Robert Bishop, *The American Clock*, E. P. Dutton & Co., Inc., New York, NY, 1976.

33. H. Bryan Rogers, private communication.

34. Eli Terry, Jr., & Co. Letterbooks, two volumes, archives of the American Clock and Watch Museum, Inc., Bristol, CT.

35. Chris Bailey, Timepiece Journal *2*, 121 (1982).

36. J. A. Whittle, "Vox Temporis," NAWCC BULLETIN, VIII, 683 (1959) ; and misplaced photo, NAWCC BULLETIN, IX, 72 (1959).

37. Collection of the NAWCC Museum, Columbia, PA.

38. Lindy Larson, private communication.

39. James C. Price, NAWCC BULLETIN, XXV, 412 (1983).

40. The Astor Galleries, *Important Sale of 191 Watches & 223 clocks — American & Foreign*, New York, NY, December 4, 1965.

41. Adolph Amend, private communication.

42. Paul Heffner, private communication.

43. Thomas Grimshaw, N A W C C BULLETIN, XX, 143 (1978).

44. *The Terry Clock Co.'s Catalogue and Price List of Terry's Patent Clocks*, Waterbury, CT, 1875, republished by the American Clock & Watch Museum, Inc., Bristol, CT, 1981, with biography of S. B. Terry by Chris Bailey.

45. Harry Williams, private communication.

46. Fred Phillippi, private communication.

47. Joe Bartels, private communication.

48. Private collection.

49. Joyce B. Wahler, private communication.

50. H. Bryan Rogers, N A W C C BULLETIN, XXVI, 267 (1984).

PHOTOGRAPHIC CREDITS
(by Figure Number)

Private Collector 1.

Joyce B. Wahler 2a, 2b, 2c, 2d, 2e.

David Taylor 3a, 3b, 11a, 11c, 12a, 12b, 12c, 15a, 15b, 15c, 17b, 17c.

Bryson Moore 4a, 4b, 4c.

Rolf Taylor 5a, 5b, 11b.

George Beals 6.

Richard Vallee 7a, 7b, 7c, 8a, 8b, 8c, 18a, 18b, 18c, 18d, 19a, 19b, 19c, 19d, 21a, 21b, 21c, 21d.

Jacque Houser 9a, 9b, 9c, 9d.

Ward Francillon 10.

H. Bryan Rogers 13a, 13b, 20a, 20b, 20c, 20d.

NAWCC Museum 14a, 14b, 14c, 14d, 16a, 16b, 16c, 16d.

Snowden Taylor 17a.

Joe Bartels 22a, 22b.

TABLE I
Time Train Tooth Counts

	Jerome's	Chauncey Jerome	Hiram Welton	Hiram Welton	Elisha Manross	Henry Terry / Silas B. Terry	The Terry Clock Co.	New Haven Clock Co.
Movement Number	1.1	2.1	31.3.2, 3.3	4.1	5.1	6.1	7.1, 7.2	8.1
1st Arbor Teeth	78*	60*	60*	80*	78*	56*	54*	78*
2nd Arbor Leaves - Teeth	6-78	8-60	8-45	10-64	8-60	8-48	9-56	8-42
3rd Arbor Leaves - Teeth	—	7-42	8-40	8-60	8-60	8-48	8-60	7-39
Escape Arbor Leaves - Teeth	6-48	7-26	8-42	8-40	7-39	8-40	7-30	8-40
Center Arbor Teeth - Leaves	36*-12	24*-10	24*-12	20*-20	12*-12	20*-12	18*-12	26*-10
Intermediate Arbor Teeth - Leaves	36-10	30- 8	36-10	40- 8	36-10	36-10	36-10	30- 8
Hour Wheel Teeth	40	32	40	48	40	40	40	32

*Mating gears between time train and motion work.

TABLE II
Strike Train Tooth Counts

	Jerome's	Chauncey Jerome	Hiram Welton	Hiram Welton	Elisha Manross	Henry Terry/ Silas B. Terry	The Terry Clock Co.	New Haven Clock Co.
Movement Number	1.1	2.1	3.1, 3.2, 3.3	4.1	5.1	6.1	7.1, 7.2	8.1
1st Arbor								
Teeth		60	60		78	56-14*	54	78
Hammer Lift Pins		—	15		—	—	—	—
2nd Arbor								
Leaves - Teeth		8-60	8-56		8-60	8-54	8-54	8-48
Hammer Lift Pins	Does not apply	2	—	Does not apply	5**	3	3	2
Count Wheel Drive Pins		2	2		5	—	3	2
Drop Slots		2	2		—	3	3	2
3rd Arbor								
Leaves - Teeth		6-50	7-45		6-60	6-48	6-60	6-48
Stop Pins		1	1			1	1	1
Fly								
Leaves		6	6		5	6	6	6
Count Wheel								
Teeth		78	78		78	52*	78	78
Slots***		12	12		12	12	12	12

*Mating gears driving count wheel.
**Also serve as count hook lift pins.
***Double width slots counted as two slots.

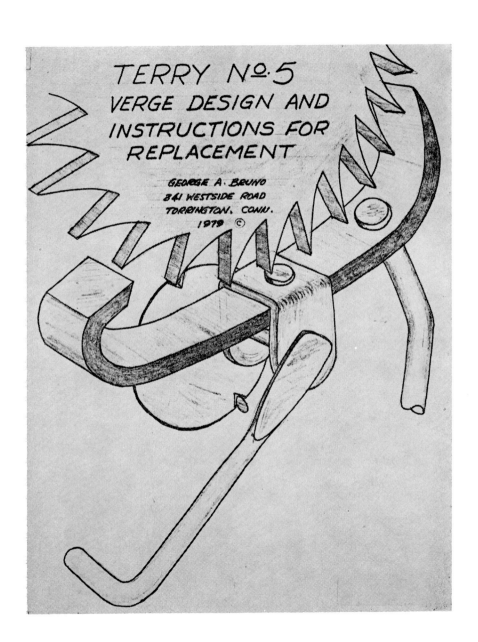

TERRY Nº.5

VERGE DESIGN AND
INSTRUCTIONS FOR
REPLACEMENT

GEORGE A. BRUNO
841 WESTSIDE ROAD
TORRINGTON, CONN.
1979 ©

THESE INSTRUCTIONS ARE DESIGNED TO ACQUAINT THE NOVICE WITH THE BASIC NOMENCLATURE AND FUNCTIONS. COMPLETION OF THE STEPS OUTLINED SHOULD PRODUCE A VERGE COMPATIBLE TO AN EXISTING ESCAPE WHEEL.

THE INSTRUCTIONS WILL BEGIN WITH NOMENCLATURE AND FUNCTIONS FOLLOWED BY DETAILED STEPS REQUIRED TO FIT A NEW VERGE AND A REVIEW OF THE IMPORTANT PORTIONS.

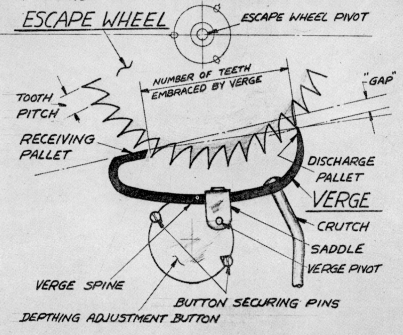

FIG. 1 ~ ESCAPE ASSEMBLY AND IDENTIFICATION

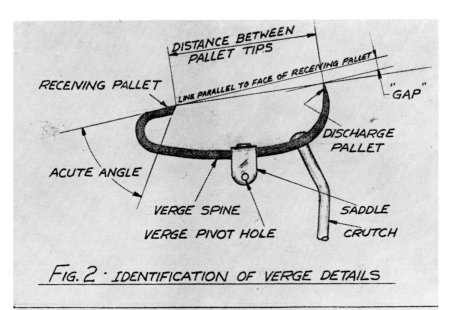

Fig. 2 · IDENTIFICATION OF VERGE DETAILS

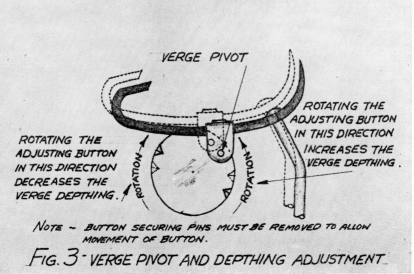

NOTE ~ BUTTON SECURING PINS MUST BE REMOVED TO ALLOW MOVEMENT OF BUTTON.

Fig. 3 ‑ VERGE PIVOT AND DEPTHING ADJUSTMENT

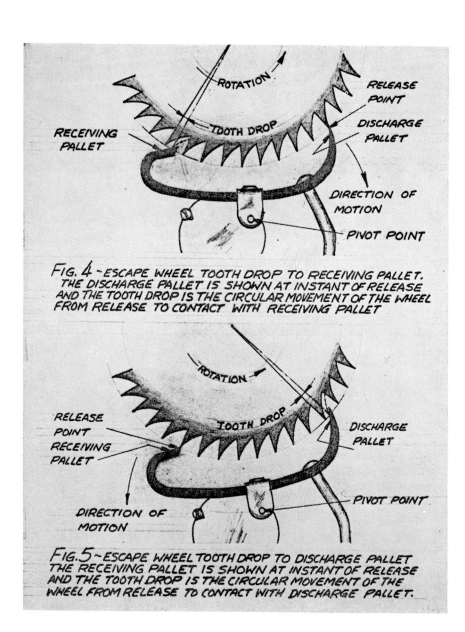

FIG. 4 ~ ESCAPE WHEEL TOOTH DROP TO RECEIVING PALLET.
THE DISCHARGE PALLET IS SHOWN AT INSTANT OF RELEASE
AND THE TOOTH DROP IS THE CIRCULAR MOVEMENT OF THE WHEEL
FROM RELEASE TO CONTACT WITH RECEIVING PALLET

FIG. 5 ~ ESCAPE WHEEL TOOTH DROP TO DISCHARGE PALLET
THE RECEIVING PALLET IS SHOWN AT INSTANT OF RELEASE
AND THE TOOTH DROP IS THE CIRCULAR MOVEMENT OF THE
WHEEL FROM RELEASE TO CONTACT WITH DISCHARGE PALLET.

THE BASIC STEPS IN FITTING A NEW VERGE ARE AS FOLLOWS :

STEP Nº. 1 - COUNT THE NUMBER OF TEETH ON THE EXISTING ESCAPE WHEEL AND REFERING TO THE TABLE BELOW, SELECT THE CORRECT NUMBER OF TEETH TO BE EMBRACED BY THE NEW VERGE. NOTE! FOR INSTRUCTIVE PURPOSES A 42 TOOTH ESCAPE WHEEL WILL BE FITTED FOR A VERGE.

NUMBER OF TEETH ON ESCAPE WHEEL	NUMBER OF TEETH TO BE EMBRACED
30 To 39	8
40 To 43	9
44 To 46	10

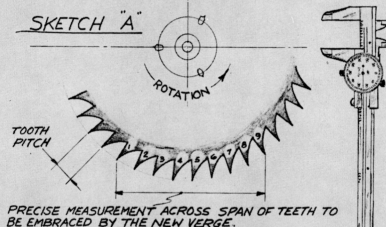

SKETCH "A"

ROTATION

TOOTH PITCH

PRECISE MEASUREMENT ACROSS SPAN OF TEETH TO BE EMBRACED BY THE NEW VERGE.

STEP Nº. 2 - WITH A 42 TOOTH ESCAPE WHEEL 9 TEETH ARE TO BE EMBRACED. MEASURE THE DISTANCE ACROSS THESE 9 TEETH WITH AN ACCURATE DIAL CALIPER OF THE TYPE SHOWN IN SKETCH "A" ABOVE. ALSO MEASURE THE TOOTH PITCH AS SHOWN AND RECORD THESE DIMENSIONS.

MEASUREMENTS TO BE USED FOR THIS LESSON AS FOLLOWS: - DISTANCE ACROSS 9 TEETH = .825" *
TOOTH PITCH = .104" *

* THESE ARE ASSUMED FIGURES FOR THIS LESSON ONLY.

STEP NO. 3 - FILE THE RECEIVING PALLET FLAT
TO APPROXIMATE PROFILE SHOW IN SKETCH "B"

SECURE VERGE BLANK IN VISE FOR ALL FILING
AND STONING OPERATIONS.

FILE THE RECEIVING PALLET BY REMOVING
¼ OF THE METAL THICKNESS.

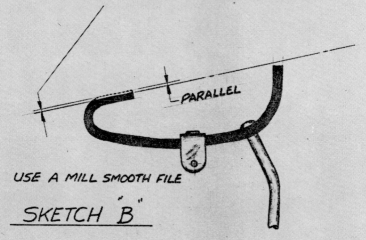

PARALLEL

USE A MILL SMOOTH FILE

SKETCH "B"

VERGE BLANK (ANNEALED)

NOTE! EXTRA MATERIAL HAS BEEN ALLOWED
AT BOTH PALLET TIPS FOR FITTING.

STEP №.4 - FILE DISCHARGE PALLET
AS DIRECTED IN SKETCH "C".

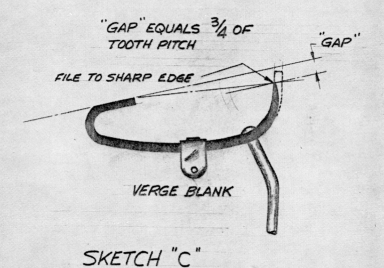

"GAP" EQUALS ¾ OF
TOOTH PITCH

"GAP"

FILE TO SHARP EDGE

VERGE BLANK

SKETCH "C"

FILE DISCHARGE PALLET TO PROFILE
SHOWN. REFER TO PAGE 5 - SKETCH "A"
FOR TOOTH PITCH DIMENSION.

STEP Nº 5 ~ FILE END OF RECEIVING PALLET
TO DIMENSIONS SHOWN IN SKETCH "D" BELOW.
THIS OPERATION IS CRITICAL AND CARE MUST BE
EXERCISED TO INSURE THE ACCURATE EXECUTION
OF THIS STEP.
  (REFER TO PAGE 5 - STEP Nº 2 FOR SOURCE OF THIS
  DIMENSION)

THE DISTANCE BETWEEN PALLET TIPS EQUALS
THE DIMENSION ACROSS SPAN OF 9 TEETH
PLUS .014"

$$
\begin{array}{r}
SO \cdot .825 \\
+ .014 \\
\hline
.839
\end{array}
$$

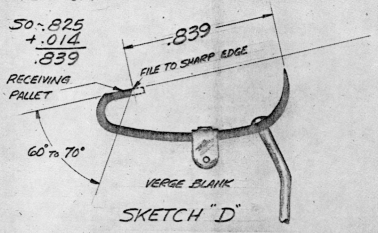

RECEIVING
PALLET

FILE TO SHARP EDGE

.839

60° TO 70°

VERGE BLANK

SKETCH "D"

FILE THE RECEIVING PALLET TO
DIMENSION SHOWN

STEP N⁰· **6** ~ THE PALLET SURFACES
MUST BE STONED SMOOTH AND POLISHED
TO REDUCE FRICTION WHEN ENGAGED TO
ESCAPE WHEEL TEETH.
(REFER TO SKETCH "E" BELOW)

MAKE CERTAIN TO LIGHTLY STONE OFF THE
SMALL BURRS THAT DEVELOP AT THE SHARP
EDGES OF THE PALLETS.

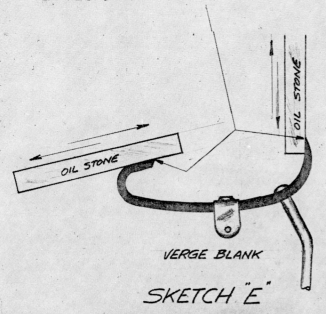

VERGE BLANK

SKETCH "E"

STONE AND POLISH PALLETS
IN DIRECTIONS SHOWN

AFTER COMPLETION OF STEP Nº 6 REAM SADDLE PIVOT HOLE
TO FIT PIVOT PIN. THIS IS A CRITICAL OPERATION SINCE THE
CLEARANCE BETWEEN THE PIVOT PIN AND THE HOLE MUST BE KEPT
TO A MINIMUM AND YET BE ABLE TO ROTATE FREELY.

THE ALIGNMENT OF THE HOLES MUST BE PRECISE · REFER TO
SKETCH "F" - REAM PIVOT HOLE THROUGH ONE LEG UNTIL IT
BARELY FITS ONTO PIVOT PIN AND THEN REAM THE PIVOT HOLE ON
THE OTHER LEG FROM OPPOSITE SIDE ·

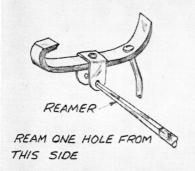

REAMER

REAM ONE HOLE FROM
THIS SIDE

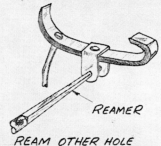

REAMER

REAM OTHER HOLE
FROM OPPOSITE SIDE

SKETCH "F"

GOOD ALIGNMENT   POOR ALIGNMENT (EXAGGERATED)

AFTER COMPLETION OF STEP Nº·6, POSITION VERGE ON PIVOT
PIN. WITH VERGE IN POSITION AND THE TWO BUTTON RETAINING
PINS REMOVED, *ADJUST FOR VERGE DEPTHING UNTIL THE RECEIVING
PALLET ALLOWS THE ESCAPE WHEEL TO HAVE A TOOTH DROP EQUAL
TO THE DROP TO THE DISCHARGE PALLET*
          REFER TO PAGE 5 - FIGURES 4 & 5
NOTE · HOLD LOWER END OF CRUTCH LIGHTLY WHILE ROTATING THE
ESCAPE ARBOR SLOWLY. THIS WILL ALLOW CRUTCH TO VIBRATE
SLOWLY UNDER CONTROL OF YOUR FINGERS TO OBSERVE THE
TOOTH DROPS. ADJUST DEPTHING IF REQUIRED.
          ~ A RULE TO REMEMBER ~
THE DISTANCE BETWEEN THE PALLET TIPS GOVERNS THE TOOTH DROP TO
THE DISCHARGE PALLET AND THE DEPTHING GOVERNS THE TOOTH DROP TO
THE RECEIVING PALLET.

AFTER THE DEPTHING ADJUSTMENT HAS BEEN COMPLETED TRY OUT THE VERGE IN ACTUAL OPERATION. WHEN SATISFIED WITH THE PERFORMANCE, REMOVE VERGE TO PREPARE FOR THE HARDENING OF THE PALLET SURFACES.

THE VERGE IS MADE OF HIGH CARBON STEEL AND BY HEATING THE PALLETS ONE AT A TIME TO A CHERRY RED COLOR WITH A PROPANE FLAME, THE VERGE MUST THEN BE QUICKLY QUENCHED IN WATER. THE PALLETS WILL NOW BE "GLASS HARD".

REPOLISH THE PALLET SURFACES AND THEN PLAY THEM ONE AT A TIME THROUGH A "GENTLE" FLAME UNTIL A LIGHT STRAW COLOR APPEARS. AT THIS POINT QUICKLY QUENCH IN WATER. THIS WILL TAME THE HARDNESS AND REDUCE THE BRITTLENESS.

THE VERGE IS NOW READY FOR USE. THE SPINE OF THE VERGE IS LEFT RELATIVELY SOFT SINCE IT WAS NOT HEATED HOT ENOUGH TO BE AFFECTED BY THE WATER QUENCH. THIS FEATURE BECOMES AN ASSET IN THE EVENT AN ERROR WAS MADE IN THE ESCAPE WHEEL OR VERGE MEASUREMENTS. THE SPINE BEING SOFT LENDS ITSELF TO BENDING TO CLOSE OR SPREAD PALLET DISTANCES SLIGHTLY.

LUBRICATE PIVOT HOLE AND PALLETS w/CLOCK OIL.

Replacing Wooden Teeth the Modern Way

Courtesy John Guerin and Space Age Technology

by Ward W. Miller (NY)

Wooden works antique clocks chronicle an interesting period in our history and many were truly works of art. But they have a common fault: a tooth on the wooden wheel is easily broken when the wood grain runs perpendicular to the tooth. The accepted method of repair requires a piece of like wood that matches the broken tooth in color and grain structure. Then the offending tooth is sawed out with a dovetail or keystone cut and a matching shape is sawed in the piece of repair wood. If you have the skill of a brain surgeon and the luck of a sweepstakes winner, the repair piece should be a sliding fit into the damaged wheel. Then the new tooth must be carefully sawed and filed to the original shape and fit. When properly executed, this procedure works well. It is also an advertisement of the craftsman's skill because the repair is obvious to the most casual observer since the grain of the wheel is always at a

Fig. 2 Wooden pinion wheel with missing teeth.

right angle to the grain of the replacement tooth.

Many of us don't have the patience or skill to do it "the old way." There must be another way . . . and there is.

You may not want to use this procedure on your priceless T. Cheney wooden clock, but the results it provides are far better than most of the dovetail work we have seen. Mr. John A. Guerin, Mid-Hudson Chapter #84 Past President, recently demonstrated at a Chapter workshop his answer to broken teeth in wooden works (Figures 1 & 2). When you have seen the results, you will agree that this is a first-class, yet simple, solution to a sometimes vexing problem. We will use modelling clay, epoxy glue, and powdered stain to create teeth that can hardly be identified from the original. And it is oh, so easy, to accomplish.

Fig. 1 Wooden wheel with one conventional repaired tooth and 2½ missing teeth.

You begin with the children's model-ling clay. It is slightly waxy and will not stick to the wood. Work it in your hands to warm and soften it, then press a large piece onto the wheel with the broken teeth, but place it on a good part of the wheel. Cover a span of teeth equal to the damaged area, plus two or three more teeth at each end of the span. This clay will become a mold for filling in the missing teeth. With your pocket knife blade flat against one side of the wheel, cut the clay away so you can see the teeth (Figure 3). Carefully pull the clay away from

Fig. 3 Children's modelling clay pattern.

the wheel. Now, replace your clay mold on the wheel so that it meshes with the good teeth and surrounds the broken teeth, creating a little dam around each missing part (Figure 4). Make sure it fits with several good teeth on either side of the missing ones.

Working with a small or pinion gear is the same (Figure 5), except that you will have to carefully pry the mold open a bit to get it off the small wheel, then bend it back into shape as you place it back on the wheel surrounding the missing teeth.

Now comes the business of manufac-turing teeth that will be difficult to identify from the original. You will need some five-minute epoxy and a selection of several different colors of dry powder stain. We found our epoxy in easy-to-use twin tubes at Radio

Fig. 4 the mold placed around the missing teeth.

Shack and the powder at Albert Con-stantine and Sons, Inc., 2050 East-chester Road, Bronx, NY 20461, but any similar material will serve you well. First, mix a small amount of the epoxy on the plastic cover that comes on a can of coffee — it won't stick to the plastic and can be easily removed later. Allow the epoxy to cure for five minutes. If it is not glass hard by then, change to a different brand or get the epoxy from a supplier who has a faster turnover on his stock. When you have found an epoxy that will set hard in five minutes, you are ready to proceed.

Fig. 5 Prying the pinion gear mold.

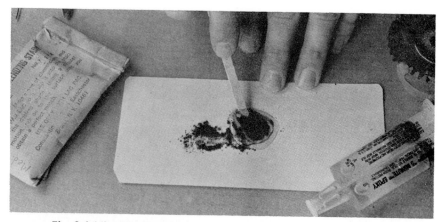

Fig. 6 Adding the powdered stain to match the original wood's color.

Fig. 7 Filling the mold.

This step is the only one that requires a little trial and error, but if you are not satisfied with the results you can always restore the wheel to its original (missing teeth) condition. Mix a small amount of the five-minute epoxy and add a small amount of the dry powder stain (Figure 6), that closely matches the original wood of the wheel. Work rather quickly in this step because we already know the epoxy will set up hard in five minutes. Use a small screwdriver to pick up some of the epoxy and work it into the mold the clay provides for the missing teeth (Figure 7). Still working quickly, ease the bubbles out of the mold and slightly over-fill each tooth cavity. Set the mold aside upright (Figure 8) so the epoxy will not

Fig. 8 Waiting for the epoxy to set.

run out, and wait about 8 to 10 minutes. While you are waiting, be sure to clean the screwdriver.

Test the epoxy to be sure it has set up hard, then pull the clay away from the wheel and you will see the wheel with its missing teeth replaced! The epoxy is very glossy, so when you dress any rough edges with your fine file, you can also smooth the flat surfaces flush with the face of the wheel and the gloss will be removed — that is why we slightly overfilled the mold. If

Fig. 9 Can you tell which teeth were replaced? They are the 3rd, 4th, and 5th to the left of the old styled wooden tooth repair.

you used just the right amount of stain, the new teeth will be indistinguishable from the original (Figure 9). If you are not pleased with the results, just grasp any new tooth with your pliers and break it away from the wheel. If you do this within 10 to 15 minutes from the original mixing, it will break clean from the wood and leave the wood as it was originally.

John Guerin showed this procedure to Jim L. Tigner, who then published it in "Inside the Clock Shop" in the July '78 issue of *Horological Times*. It is truly a creative solution, using modern materials, that takes little skill and can always be done over if the results are not pleasing.

Restoring a valuable clock to working order should be a combination of retaining as much of the original material as possible while also concealing evidence of the repair. With a little practice, the method described above provides an excellent alternative to the traditional solution.

NOTE

All photographs by the author.

From: *The Jewelers' Circular & Horological Review*, Vol. XIV, No. 2, March, 1883.

THE CLOCKMAKER'S LOCK-UP

In a certain clock factory the workmen have been separated from each other by a wire railing, thus securing their isolation, whereupon one of them relieves his over-burdened soul as follows:

On the *verge* of despair,
  tormented with rage,
My *pinions* I beat 'gainst the bars
  of my cage.
My *case* is a hard one,
  no hope of *escape*,
My *joints* all grow rusty,
  life's *mainspring* will break.
My *movements* so screwed up
  most horriby vex,
And the simplest of *actions*,
  seems highly *duplex*.
Horizontal position there's no
  room to take,

No *lever* could raise one so tied
  to the stake.
What virtue or vice,
  can a man be inspired in?
Who feels that his body,
  so closely is wired in?
I crave not for *jewels*,
  in *settings* of gold,
Give me but a *cover*,
  to keep out the cold,
A *pallet* to sleep on,
  though only of hay,
Some small store of food,
  where my *teeth may have play*.
With this quite content,
  I ne'er would complain,
For *freedom* brings pleasures and
  peace in its *train*.
But *pinned up*, without
  room for *endshake* or *play*,
The *hours* glide so slowly
  each one seems a day.
And I *watch* full of hope,
  to end this sad trial,
for old *time* to *strike*
  on eternity's *dial*.

          A. KLOKMAKER.

INTERESTING STILL COLLECTIBLE WATCHES

by James W. Gibbs (PA)

Let the reader beware. This is not an in-depth scholarly article. Rather, it is meant solely for entertainment and to suggest some types of pocket watches still possibly obtainable at reasonable prices. Unless otherwise stated they are all Swiss, late 19th or early 20th Century vintage, and bearing no notable makers' names, if any. Thus they have not yet been "discovered."

Figure 1 is a group of 8-day watches. The top one has on its dial "Majestic 8-day J. E. Caldwell & Co." The back plate is engraved "Majestic Watch Company fifteen jewels." The one at the right is unusual with date and day of week calendars and sweep seconds hand. The dial is signed "Bennett New York." The back plate is engraved "Hebdomas Watch Co. 8 days lever 6 six jewels 1 one adjustment guaranteed and replicas of 10 medals which are not explained." The real surprise is that winding causes the whole movement to revolve. So which came first — this or the Waterbury long-wind karrusel? The watches at the bottom and left are also Hebdomas with revolving movements, pin set.

Figure 2 is a group of different dials. The one at the top, at first glance, appears to be the familiar "captain's" watch. In effect it is, except it was used in French or Swiss railroad stations as one dial is marked "arrivée" the other "depart," and the dial is labeled "Gare" which is French for station. It is a lever movement claimed to contain 25 jewels made by Giroud Petron of Vevey. The watch at the right is an early digital peeping out of a beautiful painted dial. It has a 10-jewel

Fig. 1

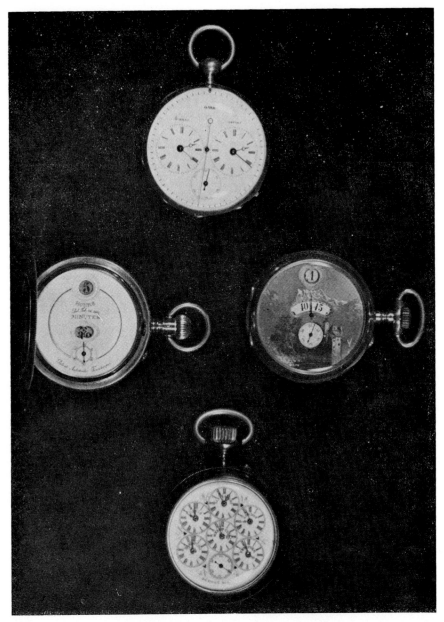

Fig. 2

cylinder escapement by Marillier Denzler of Neuveville. The bottom watch simply boasts a dial giving times in San Francisco, London, New York, Hambourg, Paris, and Mexico City. In view of this complication, the inscription "The Normal Watch" on the back plate is curious. At the left is another early digital whose dial is marked "Patent Automatic Timekeeper" and "Pat. Feb. 24, 1885." This was considered a quality watch as it is housed in a 14k gold hunting case.

Fig. 3

Fig. 4

Figure 3 illustrates several ways of interpreting time to the viewer. At the top is an early 20th Century by Draga Watch Co., 7 jewels. Hours and minutes are obviously shown by the two rotating dials. At the right is an odd one by Cyma. The long minute hand performs its job then both digital numerals advance. Why two? The dial is marked "Discus Patent." The watch on the bottom is marked "chronometre," which it isn't. Somehow the maker must have anticipated military time or men working in Alaska during the long dark months. When the button in the winding crown is depressed, the under dial disc is rotated to the right so that the black Roman numerals are supplanted by prominent red Arabic numerals 13-24. The left watch has the familiar half circle, snap-back minute hand with jump hour numeral. Inside is proclaimed the fact that this is the Modernistic patent while the dial advertises Excelsior Cigarillos.

Figure 4 is composed of examples best described as action watches. The upper left watch has a nicely painted paper dial having a small square aperture in which there is a revolving disc having tiny painted boats designed to suggest them skimming over the blue water. The upper right watch has a pretty dial with red cartouche numerals but its real zinger is the back. There a ½-inch diameter glass covered opening reveals a revolving disc boldly decorated with five 19th Century females. At lower left is a similar idea of newer vintage. When the winding crown is depressed the disc in the aperture revolves one notch bringing to view in succession seven rulers of European nations at the time of WWI. The center watch has the familiar blinking eye feature of certain desirable cast iron American clocks reduced in size and reposing in a pretty female face. At lower right is simply an example of the dummy, blind, or false pendulum.

Figure 5 proves that watches can sometimes serve more than one purpose. The watch at the upper left marked "watch barometer patent" is missing the third hand — a pointer, so the watch can serve the dual function of barometer and altimeter. The upper right watch with a 4-jewel cylinder escapement has incorporated a celsius calibrated thermometer. The center watch is a patent lever full-jeweled movement by M. I. Tobias, Liverpool, and incorporates a thermometer and tiny compass.

Fig. 5

Fig. 6

Figure 6 has a pair of easily recognized pedometer watches (or automatic winding watches). The watch at left has a heavy weight signed Godemar Freres a Geneve n 5934. The right watch has a lighter weight. The dial is signed La Fontaine 18 Palais — Royal Paris. Neither of these has any other mode of winding.

The watch in Figure 7 is some sort of a pedometer or automatic, even though that mode of winding is concealed under a bridge on which is engraved, "Semi-Self Winder C.F. Brown adjusted barrel." C. F. Brown was listed in Coventry, England, 1854. This movement can be key wound.

The watch in Figure 8 shows the beautiful silver dial with laid-on gold numerals and decorative work. The hands are magnificent. Obviously well made and probably expensive, I doubt many watches like it were sold — it weighs half a pound.

Fig. 7

Fig. 8

Fig. 9

The watches shown in Figure 9 give recognition to the always interesting repouseé cases. The upper left watch case represents Moses with the tablets containing the Ten Commandments. Appropriately, the dial has Hebrew numerals. The upper right watch is engraved but included because it shows the type of a very early monoplane such as Bleriot used in the first heavier-than-air crossing of the English Channel in 1909. It has a Roskopf escapement marked "caranti autimagnetique." The center watch case depicts the Father of our Country. The large outer oval consists of the letters U.S. in small ovals. The movement is simply engraved "Stanley Watch" and of Swiss origin. The watch case at lower left pays homage to the Wright brothers with an illustration of their famous Kitty Hawk biplane supported on the left by a hot air balloon and on the right by a Bleriot type monoplane. The movement is signed Superior Watch Co. Shown on the watch at the lower right is a coal miner surrounded by accoutrements of the trade.

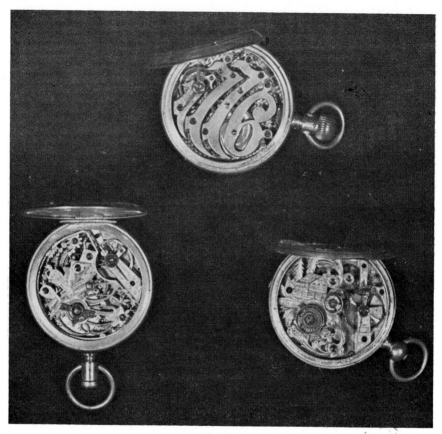

Fig. 10

The watches shown in Figure 10 bring to your attention some entrancing back plates ingeniously wrought. The top one has a 15-jewel stem wind movement with easily read bridges. As pure conjecture, watches of this sort might have been part of a Swiss exhibit of the Centennial Exhibition in Philadelphia. The back plate at lower left is more difficult to discern but essentially consists of an army bugler standing before two tents and a lot of decorative cut-out work. It is key wound and set. The lower right back plate consists of a Swiss chalet with two tall evergreen trees in the background and pretty decorative cut-out work. An additional attraction is the fact this one is crank wound and set.

We hope you have enjoyed this, and wish you luck the next time you browse through a mart or flea market.

CLOSE-UP PHOTOGRAPHY
AND HOROLOGY

by Bill Guido (OK)

Rare and historic watches often pass from one collector to another only to be secreted in a safe or bank vault for 20 more years. The researcher and cataloger of rare and unusual watches can often be greatly aided by a good clear photograph. Authors of texts on watches need clear photographs to illustrate and give life to their publications.

Near life-size photography is called macro-photography and does not require expensive equipment. A 35 mm single lens reflex camera, a tripod, a close-up accessory lens, and two desk lamps can achieve excellent results.

After obtaining a 35 mm single lens reflex camera and tripod you will need a close-up screw thread lens to fit the c a m e r a . These screw-on accessory lenses look like filters and come in diopters (strengths) of + 1,2,3,4, and 10. When screwed on a normal lens they transform it into a macro lens for under $20. Once the close-up lens is in position, a tripod or close-up stand (Figure 1) is used to position the camera above the watch. Two gooseneck incandescent lamps can be used to illuminate the movement from both sides. Using a fine grain film you focus the camera utilizing the automatic exposure meter in the camera. In a single lens reflex camera what you see is what you get, so when the image is clear, fills the viewfinder, and is correctly exposed, you will have an excellent quality photograph.

Fig. 2

Figure 2 is of a United States Watch Co., Marion, NJ, Wm. Alexander model, 18 size keywind watch with frosted and damasceened plates. This photograph was taken using a #3 diopter close-up lens and two 75-watt incandescent bulbs. Fine grain black and white film was used. Lens openings of F 8 or smaller help contrast and sharpness, w h i c h necessitates slower shutter speeds often below 1/30 second.

Figure 3 is of a Marion Watch Co., Marion, NJ, A. H. Wallis model nickel keywind. This photograph was taken using two accessory close-up lenses screwed together with a combined diopter of +13 (10+3). The enlarge-

Fig. 1

Fig. 3

ment is many times life-size, clearly showing minute details in damascening, engraving, and workmanship. We can see that a photograph of better than ten times life-size can be taken without the use of expensive macro lenses or special circular ring electronic flashes.

Figure 4 was a very difficult subject. The artwork on the United States Watch Co. dial was very faint. Using high contrast paper the resulting photo looks better than the dial itself. A combination of macro and experimentation with colored filters could have done even better.

Fig. 4

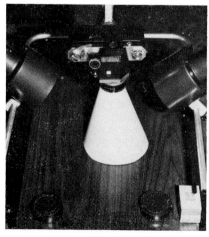

Fig. 5

Another simple technique is the use of a light diffuser (Figure 5). A piece of 8 x 11 bond paper is rolled into a cone with the small end over the camera lens and the large base over the watch. When the cone is illuminated from both sides it diffuses light evenly, thus minimizing glare spots on nickel movements, enamel dials, and watch cases.

Any enthusiast knows the pleasure derived from a new publication on watches. If these volumes were pure research without clear photographs they would be much less exciting. On page 197 of Chris Bailey's book, *Two*

Hundred Years of American Clocks and Watches, the photograph of a solid gold Presidential presentation watch brings history and beauty to life. Roy Ehrhardt's, *New Encyclopedia of American Pocket Watches*, also contains many high quality photographs of watches.

Although I have large format film capabilities as well as special macro lenses, all of the photographs in this article were taken with inexpensive accessory lenses. For further reading your local photography store can order magazines on macro photography and close-up photography.

A THIRTY-HOUR WOOD MOVEMENT CLOCK FROM THE FORESTVILLE MANUFACTURING COMPANY

by Lee H. Davis (PA)

During the summer of 1983 I received a call from a lady who owned a clock that needed a tablet painted. Upon arriving at her house I was shown the clock, which appeared to be a not too unusual 30-hour wood movement clock, lacking the tablet and having a badly flaked dial.

As I looked closer I could see the label, which was in very good condition, and I was surprised to see the clock was a product of the Forestville Manufacturing Company. I had never seen a 30-hour wood movement clock with this label and said so to the owner.

Removal of the hands and dial revealed a clean Terry-type model 5 (Figure 1) movement which was brass bushed, in agreement with the label (Figure 2). The brass bushings behind the winding arbors stood out quite plainly, and there was no sign of alterations having been made or another movement substituted for the original. This appeared to be an early Forestville Manufacturing Company product in original condition, except for the missing tablet.

Fig. 1 The brass bushed 30-hour movement. This is a 5.142 type of movement by Taylor's classification and was probably made by C. & N. Jerome.

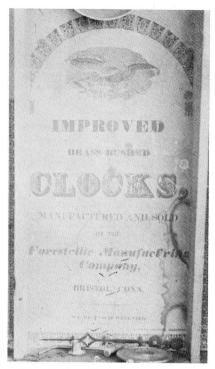

Fig. 2 The label noting the brass bushed movement. Printer was P. Canfield, Hartford.

According to Roberts, Jonathan Clark Brown came to Bristol in 1832, and by September 15 of that same year had purchased Elias Ingraham's half of the business Ingraham & Bartholomew.[1] By 1835 J. C. Brown had organized the Forestville Manufacturing Company and had commenced production of 8-day b r a s s clocks.[2] Roberts said nothing of 30-hour wood movement clock production by this firm, and apparently little or nothing has come to light on this early activity of the Forestville Manufacturing Company.

Permission was asked, and granted, to remove the clock to my home for closer inspection.

Several inquiries were made to fellow clock enthusiasts to see if they could recall ever having seen a clock

of this description by this firm. None had. I then called Stacy Wood at the NAWCC Museum to ask him to take a look at it and we set up a time to inspect the clock.

On the day I took the clock to the Museum Chris Bailey was visiting, so he looked at the clock too. Chris said he had recalled only seeing one other clock of this same description, and it was privately owned by an individual in the Bristol area.

Both Chris and I agreed that perhaps the most unusual feature of this clock is the rather long blocks below and above the stencilled half pillars (Figure 3). Although blocks at this location are not too unusual on 30-hour

Fig. 3 A 30-hour wood movement clock by Forestville Manufacturing Company. This clock is 31⅞" high, 16½" wide at the base. The tablet and dial have been repainted by the author.

wood movement clocks, these attracted our attention as they were proportioned such that it almost seemed they were made as spacers instead of decorations which added to the esthetic value of the clock. Why they were made this way is purely speculation, but the suggestion that perhaps the pillars were too short, for some reason, may not be too far from the truth.

Taking a closer look at the movement, it is almost certain that it is original to the case. Both upright supports bear only the holes intended to receive the pins which pass through the three large access holes, and there is no indication of any other movement having been there. Of course, the fact the movement is brass bushed, as the clock label says it is, helps confirm the hypothesis also.

The movement was almost certainly not made by the Forestville Manufacturing Company, but was most likely a product of one of the prolific movement making firms in the Bristol area in the early 1830's . . . very likely Jeromes & Darrow, or C. & N. Jerome.

Using Taylor's Terry type movement key[3] the following characteristics lead to those movements classified as sub-type 5.142. Movements in this category have the following characteristics:

1. The strike wires are not centered with respect to the access hole.

2. The holes for the count wheel drop hook are small, large, small.

3. The count wheel retainer wire is positioned at 4:30.

4. The escape wheel bridge has a rectangular tip.

5. The front strike wire pivot material is W/W (wood/wood).

6. The verge pin button is round.

7. Access holes are large. (Larger than 9/16".)

8. There is not a square hour shaft and clutch on the intermediate wheel.

9. There are rings or cups around the front plate strike wire pivots.

10. There are bushings around the winding arbors, but no rings or cups.

Although Taylor does not list any primary makers for 5.142 movements, he does list Jeromes & Darrow as the makers of 5.112 movements, and the only major difference in these is the SSS holes in 5.112 types and the SLS holes in the 5.142 movements.

According to Roberts, Jeromes & Darrow were in operation from 1828-1833, and they produced a variety of movements, including 30-hour wood movements with the improved brass bushings.[4] They were known to have sold their movements, or traded them, to other clock companies in the Bristol area, as well as case makers. Taylor has located 5.142 type movements in clocks that bear the following labels: John Bacon; Marsh, Williams & Co.; Orton, Preston & Co.; Addison Johnson; Case, Gilbert & Co.; Williams, Orton, Preston's & Co.; L. Smith & A. Blakesley; George Mitchell; Henry Hart; T. M. Roberts; Terry & Andrews; Conant & Sperry; C. & N. Jerome; Henry A. Miller; Crum & Barber.

Inspection of the above list reveals that as far as is presently known, none of these firms, with the exception of C. & N. Jerome, were movement makers. Each firm contracted for its movements, as apparently the Forestville Manufacturing Company did in its infancy.[5]

An interesting side question might be how the Forestville Manufacturing Company came to be using a Jeromes & Darrow movement (if this is indeed a Jeromes & Darrow movement) when Jeromes & Darrow were out of business by 1833, and the Forestville Manufacturing C o m p a n y was not organized under that name until 1835. If the movement was not from Jeromes & Darrow, then it must have been a product of Chauncey & Noble Jerome who continued on from 1833-1839.[6]

Looking at the movement in more detail shows the dimensions of the plates measure 8⅛" high by 6½" wide, with plate width being 5/16". Distance between plates is 1¾". Both the front and back plate appear to be of oak with all wheels and the fly bushed with brass on the front plate, and all but the great wheels bushed in brass on the back plate.

No other significant features were noticed. The wheel counts are as follows:

Those familiar with Terry movements will notice the wheel count is exactly like the Terry Standard Model 5 movements, and in fact the train layout is very close to the Terry movement. Differences are mainly in the details outlined in the above characteristic table which delineates this as a 5.142 sub-type movement.[7]

TIME TRAIN

Wheel	teeth	pinion	
Great wheel	36	—	(winds clockwise)
Second wheel	48	8	
Third wheel	36	8	(mates with motion work)
Fourth wheel	32	8	
Escape wheel	32	8	

MOTION WORK

Center arbor	40	9	
Intermediate	36	12	
Hour wheel	36	—	

STRIKE TRAIN

Great wheel	36	—	(winds counterclockwise)
Second wheel	36	9	(has secondary 6 pinions through front plate to drive count wheel, and 9 lift pins on the wheel)
Third wheel	36	8	(2 drop slots on wheel)
Fourth wheel	36	6	(1 warning pin)
Fan	—	6	

ACKNOWLEDGEMENT

A special thanks to Bob Kefauver of Blatner's Photography Studio, York, PA, for the photography.

REFERENCES

1. *The Contributions of Joseph Ives to Connecticut Clock Technology: 1810-1862,* by Kenneth D. Roberts, published by the American Clock and Watch Museum, Bristol, CT, 1970, p. 141.

2. Roberts, p. 141.

3. "Characteristics of S t a n d a r d Terry-Type 30 Hour Wooden Movements as a Guide to Identification of Movement Makers," by Snowden Taylor. NAWCC BULLETIN No. 5, Vol. XXII, October, 1980, p. 455.

4. *Eli Terry and the Connecticut Shelf Clock,* by Kenneth D. Roberts. Published by the Ken Roberts Publishing Company, Bristol, CT, 1973, p. 138.

5. Taylor, on page 443, outlines those firms or individuals he considers to be actual movement makers. C. & N. Jerome would fall under Chauncey Jerome and his firms.

6. Roberts, in his book on Eli Terry (#4 above), lists Jeromes & Darrow as being in business from 1827-1833, and C. & N. Jerome from 1833-1839, p. 296.

7. For a more detailed look at Eli Terry's standard Model 5 movement, see ''T e r r y Standard Thirty-Hour Wood Movement Contemporaries,'' by A. Bruce Burns. NAWCC BULLETIN 149, Vol. XIV, December 1970, p. 734.

COUNTING WATCH JEWELS

by John W. Grass (CA)

HOMINYJOOLSITGOT: That is the secret password of watch collectors. This jungle cry stands for "How many jewels does your watch have?" The number of jewels in a watch is one sign of its quality, so collectors look for watches with lots of jewels.

Have you ever wondered how an experienced collector can almost immediately determine the number of jewels in a watch? The hope here is to teach you this art. The first hint is to look and see if the maker marked his watch with the jewel count. If you want to learn more, then read on.

Just as the wheels of your car turn on bearings, so do the wheels in clocks and watches turn on bearings. The bearings used in clocks and watches are usually made from brass or sapphire. In most clocks, the bearings are made by simply drilling holes of the proper size into the brass plates. If the loads on the clock wheels are small and the pivots are polished, these brass bearings are completely satisfactory.

Although the friction between a steel pivot and a brass bearing is very small, the friction between a steel pivot and a jewelled bearing is even smaller. Brass bearings may last for centuries without too much wear, but the wear on jewelled bearings is almost non-existent. Jewels are used in watches so they will run with less energy, run with greater timing accuracy, and run without showing signs of wear.

Some jewelled bearings are made with straight holes, and the pivots which turn in them have shoulders; these are called *Plate Jewels*. The holes in the jewels support the pivots and the shoulders limit the amount of length-wise motion of the axle. Balance staff pivots are described as conical. Instead of the pivot ending with a shoulder, balance staff pivots terminate with a rounded flare. Special *Balance Hole Jewels* with curved back sides are used to support balance wheel pivots. The end-shake of the balance wheel is controlled with flat jeweles called *End Stones* or *Cap Jewels*. Four jewels (two hole jewels and two cap jewels) are required to support a balance wheel. Only two jewels are required to support the ordinary wheels.

Not all jewels in watches are bearings; there are also some specialized jewels. In watches with lever escapements, the fork bats the balance wheel back and forth by hitting the *Roller Jewel* mounted on the balance staff. The roller jewel is a D-shaped pin. The escape wheel, in lever watches, applies power to the fork by sliding down the faces of a couple rectangular stones called *Pallet Jewels*. Other types of escapements in both clocks and watches have their special jewels.

Getting back to watches and counting the jewels: seven is the minimum number of jewels a "jeweled watch" can have. It should have two balance hole jewels, two cap jewels for the balance, one roller jewel on the balance staff, and the two pallet jewels which engage the escape wheel. You can spot seven-jewel watches by finding the jewel on the balance cock, and noticing that none of the other wheels turn in jewels.

Jewels are usually added in pairs. On rare occasions you may find a nine-jewel watch with the escape wheel turning in jewels. More usually, the next step up from seven jewels are the fifteen-jewel watches. If you can see the jewels at each of the wheel pivots, but none on the center wheel, the jewel count probably is fifteen. Warning! As was mentioned, the number of jewels is a sign of quality and

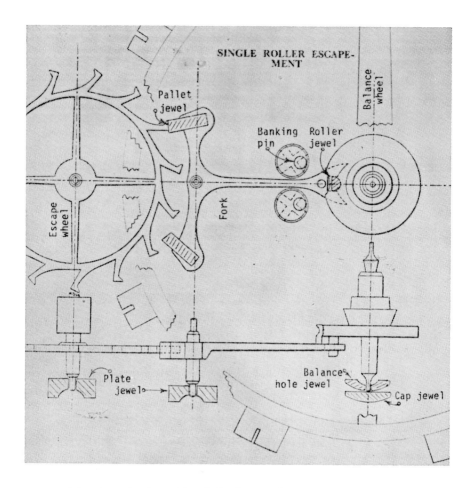

SINGLE ROLLER ESCAPE-MENT

Pallet jewel

Banking pin

Roller jewel

Balance wheel

Escape wheel

Fork

Plate jewel

Balance hole jewel

Cap jewel

some watchmakers simply put jewels in the top plate where you can see them and none on the other side, where they would be just as important. The clue here is the size of the jewels; if they are uncommonly large, suspect they are meant to be seen and the watch has only eleven jewels.

When the center wheel is also jewelled, the jewel count probably is at least seventeen and the watch is of high quality. The next step is to look for additional cap jewels. Remember the arrangement of the four jewels which support the balance wheel? This same treatment can be applied to the escape wheel pivots to give us nineteen jewels, and also to the pivots of the fork for twenty-one jewels. The way to spot cap jewels is to look for jewels without holes.

Twenty-three-jewel watches are a lot less common than the ones with twenty-one. They usually have jeweled mainspring barrels. These jewels are easy to spot because they are very large (and expensive to make) and are set in the middle of the mainspring ratchet wheel. There are, however, exceptions; the Waltham jewelled barrel has internal jewels which can't be seen, but the engraving on the watch will say "23 jewels." Both Hamilton and Elgin made nineteen-jewel watches which had jewelled barrels — an expensive way to add two jewels. Waltham also made twenty-one-jewel watches with jewelled barrels and no caps on the fork. Howard made twenty-three-jewel watches with jewels for banking pins.

Beyond twenty-three jewels, the counting gets tricky. The additional jewels are mainly for show and the maker surely has marked the jewel count on the watch. If we can add cap jewels to the escape wheel, then why not also to the fourth wheel? The bottom pivot of the fourth wheel carries the second hand and obviously can't have a cap jewel, but that doesn't stop putting one on the top end to give a count of twenty-four jewels. We can also do this to the third wheel for twenty-five jewels, or to both ends of the third wheel for twenty-six jewels.

Using lots of jewels makes a good impression and encourages customers to buy watches. Since the customer doesn't know how to find the jewels anyhow, why not just claim lots of jewels? This too has been done; do a fancy engraving job, use a name that sounds familiar, and claim twenty-one or twenty-three jewels for an inferior seven-jewel watch. This, however, violates the law. Waltham made one hundred-jewel watches by simply sticking one hundred jewels in one place or another. The law was then changed to read "functional jewels."

Of course, it is possible to have a very fine watch with desirable attachments like repeaters and chronographs, and to sensibly jewel it and get a jewel count of more than thirty. This is being pointed out so you don't discard a complicated Patek Philippe as a fake because it has too many jewels.

Several American watch factories built fine watches with up to twenty-three jewels. Some also built watches with up to twenty-eight jewels, but I doubt the extra jewels did anything to improve the running of the watch. It is, however, fun for us watch collectors to try to find these high jewelled watches, and we pay dearly for this fun.

STATEMENT OF OWNERSHIP, MANAGEMENT AND CIRCULATION

As required by Act of August 12, 1970; Section 3685, Title 39, United States Code

1. TITLE OF PUBLICATION: Bulletin of the National Association of Watch and Clock Collectors, Inc. 2. DATE OF FILING: October 1, 1984. 3. FREQUENCY OF ISSUE: Six times a year. 4. LOCATION OF KNOWN OFFICE OF PUBLICATION: 514 Poplar St., Columbia, PA 17512. 5. LOCATION OF THE HEADQUARTERS OR GENERAL BUSINESS OFFICES OF THE PUBLISHERS (Not printers): 514 Poplar St., Columbia, PA 17512. 6. NAMES AND ADDRESSES OF PUBLISHER, EDITOR, AND MANAGING EDITOR: Publisher, National Association of Watch and Clock Collectors, Inc., 514 Poplar St., Columbia, PA 17512. (Printed by the Mifflin Press, Inc., 336 Locust St., Columbia, PA 17512.) Editor: Terence M. Casey, 514 Poplar St., Columbia, PA 17512. Managing Editor, None. 7. OWNER: National Association of Watch and Clock Collectors, Inc., 514 Poplar St., Columbia, PA 17512. 8. KNOWN BONDHOLDERS, MORTGAGES, AND OTHER SECURITY HOLDERS OWNING OR HOLDING 1 PERCENT OR MORE OF TOTAL AMOUNT OF BONDS, MORTGAGES OR OTHER SECURITIES: None. 9. THE PURPOSE, FUNCTION AND NONPROFIT STATUS OF THIS ORGANIZATION AND THE EXEMPT STATUS FOR FEDERAL INCOME TAX PURPOSES have not changed during the preceding 12 months. 10. EXTENT AND NATURE OF CIRCULATION: A. TOTAL NUMBER OF COPIES PRINTED — Average of preceding 12 months: 32,814. Actual number of copies of single issue published nearest to filing date: 32,000. B. PAID CIRCULATION: (1) Sales through dealers and carriers, street vendors and counter sales: None. (2) Mail subscriptions: 31,887. C. TOTAL PAID CIRCULATION: 31,887. D. FREE DISTRIBUTION BY MAIL, CARRIER OR OTHER MEANS: Samples, complimentary, and other free copies: 23 to major museums and libraries. E. TOTAL DISTRIBUTION (Sum of C and D): 31,910. F. COPIES NOT DISTRIBUTED: (1) Office use, left over, unaccounted, spoiled after printing: 904. (2) Returns from news agents: None. G. TOTAL (Sum of E, F1 and 2): 32,814.

I certify that the statements made by me above are correct and complete.

Terence M. Casey, Editor

1984 CONVENTION
INDIANAPOLIS, IN

by Rick Weber (IN)

Our 40th National Convention was conducted by members of Host Chapters 18 and 26 who deserve far more than just "thanks" for their commitment. The committee heads and workers adopted the attitude of "Let's go beyond mere adequacy and make this an outstanding Convention." Based on the 6"-high stack of complimentary letters received, these hard-working people succeeded in that goal. Their efforts far exceeded my expectations as General Chairman, and I am very proud of their achievements.

A summary of the Convention highlights includes:

- The lowest registration fees in eight years were charged.
- The walk-in registration was the largest ever for an NAWCC National, with the second-largest total attendance, 2,450.
- The mart was the largest ever conducted at an NAWCC event, offering 760 8' tables and drive-in access to the mart hall.
- Free meals were offered to all participants and guests at the President's Breakfast, Old Timers' and Fellows' Luncheon, and Post Convention Breakfast.
- And, financially speaking, the 1984 Convention still finished well "in the black."

Attendance exceeded 2,450, making the 1984 Convention second in size only to the 1980 Convention in Boston. Outstanding Convention facilities and a centralized location contributed to this large participation.

Attendees of the 1984 Convention saw the largest NAWCC mart ever. Seven hundred sixty tables — each 8' long instead of the usual 6' — filled a well-lighted hall the size of two football fields. That comes out to one and one quarter miles of tables! Table holders, weary in years past of unloading at smelly dumpster docks and carting valuables on bakery racks thru mazes of halls and elevators, were pleasantly surprised to find they were welcome to drive into our hall to within a few feet of their tables. A well-organized team of traffic controllers insured an efficient safe flow of vehicles in and out of the hall.

In the center of the mart hall was the Administration Booth, commanded by the indefatigable Mart Chairman Carl Wiesenberg, where messages, announcements, lost and found, and a variety of other functions were performed. Also located at the center were promotional displays for up-coming NAWCC National Conventions.

The workshop areas for the '84 Convention were set up in the mart hall and also in a separate, smaller room off the main lobby. Dr. Fred Beeler gave lectures on escapements, and Cindy Burleigh Servino demonstrated gold leafing in the quieter small room. The larger workshop area in the mart hall was a constant source of activity. Ted Crom was on hand much of the time to demonstrate his huge collection of antique horological tools. Ted McDuffie demonstrated wheel cutting tools and techniques to anyone interested and was kept very busy most of the time. Louis Vuille gave fascinating demonstrations of jewel piercing using a 19th Century Swiss jewelling lathe. Vic Cheal showed many attendees techniques and materials used in restoring old clock cases.

Speakers for the 1984 NAWCC National Convention included Chris Bailey, an NAWCC Fellow and Managing Director of the American Watch and Clock Museum, who gave a slide presentation on this prestigious museum. Philip Balcomb, a Fellow of

NAWCC and frequent contributor to the BULLETIN, presented, "An Evolution of a Clock Collection." Dana Blackwell, also a Fellow and Past First Vice-President of NAWCC, gave a slide talk on "The History of Patek Philippe and Geneva Watchmaking."

Theodore Crom, a past Director and Fellow of NAWCC as well as several European horological societies, lectured on "Antique Horological Shop Tools." Dr. William C. Heilman, a recognized authority on Howard watches, presented the histories behind a fabulous collection of presentation watches which were on display in the exhibit room. Catherine Lippert, Associate Curator of Decorative Arts at the Indianapolis Museum of Art, spoke on the subject of the Ruth Allison Lilly Collection of Watches.

Dorothy Mastricola, Senior Lecturer of the world-famous Time Museum in Rockford, gave a "slide tour" through that facility. William Meggers, Jr., a well-known watch historian, gave us a slide presentation on the "History and Products of the Illinois Watch Company." Suzzane Smart, Director of Public Relations at the Indianapolis Children's Museum, lectured on the subject of "How Chapters can Help with Fund Raising for the NAWCC Museum." And, William Smith, an

internationally-recognized horological craftsman, gave a dissertation accompanied by slides on "Making and Constructing a Grasshopper Skeleton Clock."

The 1984 Convention auction, under the direction of Jim Cridge, ran smoothly as 120 horological items were put up for sale. Much credit should also be given to Auctioneer Bobby Webber, who once again came through with a fine performance.

The exhibit room housed several horological displays including antique calendar clocks, Black Forest clocks, Gruen Watch Company watches and related memorabilia, modern reproductions of woodworks clocks, horological museum literature, and Westclox clocks and advertising material. Also displayed were a variety of exhibits featuring reproduction and restoration

Shorty LaRose (left) and Tom LaRose present the Banquet Grand Prize — a Burleigh Presentation Banjo — to Mrs. William Aitken of Terre Haute. ——>

Bob Gruen with his display of Gruen watches. A member of this famous watchmaking family, Bob also exhibited much Gruen memorabilia.

591

Top, from left to right: Bobby Webber, Auctioneer; Elizabeth Weber; Rhea Oshier; Jim Cridge, Auction Chairman; and Rudi Kamper. The bottom two photos combined show only about half of the mart hall. Over 1¼ miles of tables with 10-feet wide aisles covered a floor the size of two football fields.

A fascinating display of wood movement clocks, hand-crafted by Robert Hatch.

Jim Baxter and a few of his antique calendar clocks. Mr. Baxter made available 70 models from his fabulous collection for the '84 Convention Exhibit of Calendar Clocks.

services offered by contemporary craftsmen. The Time Museum in Rockford, IL, compiled a fascinating horological exhibit. Add to all this the Achievement Awards display of 41 hand-crafted horological items, and the door prize booth, and you can see why the exhibit room was a buzz of activities.

The Antique Calendar Clock Exhibit featured 90 American examples — all of museum quality. The lion's share of this display was provided by Jim Baxter, whose generosity and efforts in setting up the display were very much appreciated.

The Westclox display was the most comprehensive collection of Westclox clocks and literature ever assembled. The exhibit and accompanying booklet were the culmination of several years of research, collecting, and restoration by Bill Stoddard and Richard Tjarks.

Bob Gruen put together an outstanding exhibit of Gruen Watch Company timepieces and memorabilia. He was present much of the time to answer questions a b o u t the family-owned business.

A rare and valuable collection of presentation watches was also included in the exhibit room. The owner of these fine timepieces, Dr. William Heilman, gave a slide presentation detailing the history behind each watch.

Roy Ehrhardt placed some of his horological patent models in our showcases. These unique pieces are rarely seen, and we appreciate Roy's loan of his collection.

A portion of the exhibit room was devoted to examples of reproduction and restoration services and reproduction parts by modern craftspersons. These included a display of reverse-painted tablets by Lee Davis, reproduction woodworks components by Donald Bruno, gold leafing and a presentation banjo by Ted Burleigh and Cindy Servino, reverse glass painting and stenciling by Margaret Watts, and reverse-painted tablets by Karl Barathy.

Master craftsman Bob Hatch displayed six of his reproduction woodworks clocks and two of his own design — a weight-driven wood movement to fit in a Willard-style banjo case and a three-train, all-wood mechanism that played the full Westminster chimes. Mr. Hatch also displayed a reproduction Terry box case shelf clock with an open strap wood works movement in the Achievement Award Contest, for which he received First Place in the Best Reproduction category.

Also included in the exhibit room was a fascinating display of Black Forest clocks that i n c l u d e d rare spring-driven shelf versions, all from the collection of Glenn Seeds. Mr. Seeds and his wife, Julia, with the help of Imogene Spaulding, also organized the Door Prize function of the Convention.

Tours for the 1984 Convention were organized by Dorothy Jones and included a n o s t a l g i c journey back through 150 years to the Conner Prairie Pioneer Settlement. After visiting the log homes and workshop of 1836 Indiana pioneers, a meal was served with foot-stompin' traditional music provided by the Country Sunshine Band. Another tour to Historic Lockerbie Square included visits to James Whitcomb Riley's Victorian home and Don Bollinger's 19th Century clock and watch shop.

The "Hoosier Hospitality Suite" was

Karl Barathy proudly displays his 1984 N A W C C National Convention Limited Edition Clock, one given at each banquet table.

one of the highlights of the '84 Convention. In the early stages of planning, Chairperson Mary Carroll promised that she and her fellow workers would make this function much more than just an obligatory fulfillment of National Convention requirements. Those who attended found how well Mary and her assistant Mable Urschel and all hospitality workers succeeded. Instead of opening the doors for a few hours a day — as is usual practice — the Hospitality Room remained open during the entire Convention, offering at no charge an inexhaustible supply of beverages and home-made baked goods. (After baking 5,000 cookies, they quit keeping count!) These were served not only to walk-in guests but also delivered to those in the mart hall who were handicapped or unable to leave their tables.

NAWCC members enjoyed other offerings of our Hoosier Hospitality Suite including safety pins, bandaids, aspirin, magazines, and newspapers. A committee person was always on hand to disperse friendly advice about what to see and places to dine in downtown Indianapolis. The tireless efforts of these hospitality hosts and hostesses added greatly to the success of the '84 Convention.

From left to right: Dave Hanna, Pre-registration and Co-Chairman; Fred Linker, Co-Chairman; Rick Weber, General Chairman.

Our banquet — the final event of the 1984 Convention — saw 700 in attendance Saturday night. Following a delicious roast beef dinner, we were all entertained by the songs and antics of the Ripscord Four Barbershop Quartet. President Gene Bagwell summarized NAWCC activities for the past year and presented special awards and fellowships.

Mrs. William Aitken of Terre Haute, IN, was the happy recipient of the Banquet Grand Prize — a Burleigh Presentation Banjo clock. This generous donation was presented by Shorty LaRose of S. LaRose, Inc. Other prizes included a Henley carriage clock donated by Manfred Trauring, and 70 limited edition '84 Convention clocks made available, one at each table, by Karl Barathy. The Host Chapters, 18 and 26, presented silk flower arrangements to one lucky person at each table.

Retiring Editor of the BULLETIN, Dr. Douglas H. Shaffer, was honored for his ten years of service to NAWCC in that position. Dr. Shaffer introduced our new Editor, Terry Casey, to the NAWCC members present.

It is our hope that a new spirit of cooperation among organizers of present and future NAWCC National Conventions was started in Indianapolis. Directors of future NAWCC Nationals were given red carpet treatment and issued staff badges that gave them "free run" of our event. Our committee heads offered a lot of advice and help to these persons in the planning of their Conventions. For example, much of our structures and signs will be used again in Atlanta next year. The ultimate result should be a saving of money and reduction in the number of mistakes repeated because future Convention organizers were not informed of them.

A special "Thank You" from the members of Chapters 18 and 26 goes out to all of you who attended and helped make the 1984 NAWCC National Convention one of the best ever!

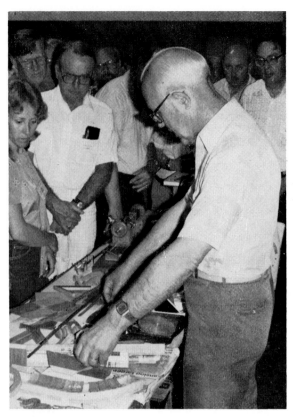

Victor Cheal demonstrates clock cabinet restoration techniques in the Workshop Area; Louis Vuille demonstrates watch jewel piercing using an antique Swiss jewelling lathe; and Ted McDuffie gives a workshop demonstration of wheel and pinion cutting and instructions for making fly cutters.

1984 NAWCC
CRAFT CONTEST

by Karl E. Hoke (MD)

Twenty horological items, the fruits of the work-benches of some of America's finest craftsmen, were singled out for honors at the 1984 NAWCC Convention in Indianapolis, IN.

Contest Chairman Foster Campos said the "quality in workmanship" in the seven categories was an outstanding feature of the Indianapolis competition. Reverse paintings, clock cases, and reproduction entries in the horological craft contest were outstanding.

The forty-one entries in the craft event came from seventeen states and Sussex, England. The craft exhibit was complemented and enhanced by six non-competitive exhibits from Michigan, Tennessee, Ohio, Iowa, and New Jersey. Some of the six non-competitive exhibits were winners in previous craft shows.

Fig. 1

TOP ENTRIES IN THE SEVEN CATEGORIES

EXCELLENCE IN WORKMANSHIP

1st   Gerhard M. Hutter, FL, Skeleton clock
                      (see Figure 1)
2nd Harold H. Hellman, IL, Skeleton clock
3rd Richard L. Givler, OH, Vienna type escapement
     movement

BEST BRASS MOVEMENT

1st   Clarence A. Sisco, NC, Crystal wheel clock
                      (see Figure 2)
2nd Howard W. Klein, MO, 3-dial English regulator

BEST WOOD CASE

1st   Robert E. VanderHoeven, NY, Vienna
     regulator (see Figure 3)
2nd Edwin H. Hall, MD, Lyre clock
3rd Edmund H. Anthon, Jr., OH, Ithaca hanging
     Belgrade

BEST REPRODUCTION

1st   Robert W. Hatch, IN, Eli Terry 1816 strap
     movement in box case (see Figure 4)
2nd Arthur E. Wallmark, MD, Ithaca perpetual
     calendar #3
3rd Harry A. Goodrick, MI, Congreve rolling ball
     clock

BEST PAINTING (Dial or Glass)

1st   Ann M. Bannister, MA, Reverse painting —
     Boston State House (see Figure 5)
2nd Victor J. Cross, FL, Banjo glasses
3rd Leonard W. Rutlin, FL, Banjo glasses

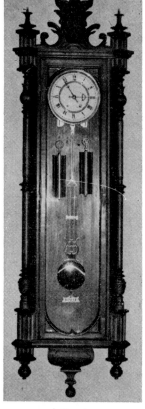

Fig. 3

Fig. 2

Fig. 4

Fig. 5

BEST TOOL
1st   William R. Smith, TN, Mainspring tool
2nd   Robert G. Fortman, NY, Atmos clock tools
3rd   Robert J. McGinness, NY, Jig for cutting clock
        wheels

NOVELTY CLASS
1st   Michael A. Paul, OH, Miniature double-dial
        calendar clock
2nd   Jacques Deveau, NY, Aaron Willard clock
3rd   Graham P. Cross, GA, Miniature wall regulator

SIGHT IMPAIRED MEMBERS

interested in the

BULLETIN ON CASSETTE TAPES

contact NAWCC Headquarters.

NAWCC STAFF

Name	Title	Additional Duties
HEADQUARTERS: 717-684-8261		
Stacy B. C. Wood, Jr.	*Administrator/Museum Director*	(Museum Donations, Guest Speakers)
Thelma Farley	*Administrative Assistant*	(Chapter Services)
Beverly A. Rutt	*Treasurer's Assistant*	
Pamela J. Lindenberger	*HQ Data Processor*	(Membership Services
Allan R. Kulman	*Shipping Clerk*	
EDITORIAL: 717-684-5544		
Terence M. Casey	*Editor*	
Amy J. Smith	*Associate Editor*	(Programs)
Ruth B. Simmons	*Editorial Assistant*	(Chapter Highlights, Lending Library)
MUSEUM: 717-684-8261		
Bruce G. Shoemaker	*Museum Development Director*	
Donald J. Summar	*Librarian*	(Research Library)
Patricia A. Tomes	*Registrar*	
Elaine P. Menchey	*Head Museum Guide*	(Museum Tours)
Elmira S. Kise	*Museum Guide*	

BUSINESS HOURS
Headquarters: Monday-Thursday, 8-5; Friday, 8-4; Saturday & Sunday, closed.
Museum: Monday-Friday, 9-4; Saturday, 9-5; Sunday, closed.

MYSTERY
MOSTLY
SOLVED

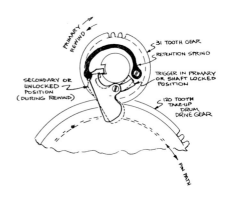

by Robert E. Reichel (WA)

"A horse, a horse, my kingdom for a horse." These words by Shakespeare signified a pleading cry. I likewise had a critical need, as published in the December 1983 BULLETIN, under the title "Mystery Clock From Australia." You will recall I had purchased a Vienna Regulator perpetual calendar clock in Australia, which had all the local experts baffled as to how to make it operate automatically in the date ribbon rewind mode.

The article was responded to by 21 BULLETIN readers and members from 12 U.S. states and 3 foreign countries. These readers reported 15 ownings and sightings of identical or similar clock movements. Six members went to considerable effort to describe the clocks/calendar detail operation. Ironically, several letters confessed to having identical ribbon problems. Almost all who reported movement problems, professed to having a similar task to conquer, that of finding suitable ribbon replacement material. Only in a few cases had a successful replacement been made, and then with rough linen rather than the original material of silk. A source for $1\frac{1}{2}''$ to $1\frac{7}{8}''$ wide by 84" long silk ribbon has eluded everyone. One other element of the "Mystery Clock" remains unsolved, that was an understanding of the pendulum engraving (see Figure 6, p. 690, December 1983 BULLETIN). The Latin inscription was explained but not the significance of the motif of the decoration.

In the resolution of the errant rewind mechanism, I was startled by one writer's assertion that the lock spring on the trigger of the 31-tooth gear was not original and should be discarded! See Figure 18, p. 697, original article. My even closer examination convinced me that the workmanship and design were in full agreement with the rest of the mechanism. Another reader marginally suggested the need to insure a *light* spring action. So maybe this was the answer. A series of experimental adjustments did prove the latter to be correct.

The spring proved to have a two-position action. One to *hold* the lock trigger in the shaft key slot, until thrown out by a pin on the take-up drum. The second action happens by a mathematical relationship between the 31-tooth gear and a pin on the 120-tooth gear counter-rotating during rewind, relocking the trigger so month day "1" is in the aperature.

The clock was probably made sometime between 1890 and 1910 by Gebrüder Wilde, Uhrenfabric, Villingen, Baden, Schwartzwald.

In addition to English lettering on the week, day, and month name drums, they also used German and Portugese.

I want to thank all of those writing to me for their interest, and especially the BULLETIN Editorial staff for forwarding the letters.

THE NAWCC MUSEUM

514 Poplar Street, Box 33, Columbia, PA 17512 — Phone (717) 684-8261

Museum Hours:
Monday-Friday, 9-4; Saturday, 9-5;
Closed Sundays and Thursday, November 22nd.

Stacy B. C. Wood, Jr., Museum Director

MUSEUM AND RESEARCH CENTER

Dear fellow members:

As a new arrival to the NAWCC Museum let me send greetings and express my appreciation for your support of the capital fund drive. After serving as the curator and administrator of a decorative arts museum and as past president of the Museum Council of Lancaster County, I have in the past eight years become familiar with the NAWCC, Inc. I commend your Director, Stacy Wood, your Trustees, and you, the membership, for operating one of the most professional museums in the country.

It is a challenge to serve as Development Officer in such a vital campaign, and vital it is. The proposed expansion of your Museum is no frivolous affair. It is not a case of a Director or Trustees wishing to expand simply to obtain state of the art facilities. Nor does it spring from a "grow or die" philosophy. Rather, the Museum stands at a critical point. It is at present, unable to fulfill its responsibility of preserving and presenting for study a host of important timepieces, irreplaceable collections, and vital research data — unable because it lacks space, and much of its unique wealth lies crated in storage, off site, out of reach in much less than optimum climate.

Your Museum is the finest repository of horological information in the United States. To preserve and present this material, it must expand. It needs the total commitment of the entire membership, however, to raise the $1,500,000 for the needed Museum and Research Center. The $500,000 necessary for construction will not be spent until there is a $1,000,000 endowment to pay for the increased operational costs such an expansion entails. The Museum must always be an asset, not a yearly drain; therefore, any expansion must be self-supporting.

To date, we have raised in pledges or gifts, large and small, $263,000 from our Chapters and over 1,900 of our 32,500 members. It is my hope, and that of these donors, that this campaign will be successful as a result of a large display of support from many members, contributing whatever amount they may be able.

So that you are aware of our campaign program let me add that grant applications have been sent to the National Endowment for the Humanities, Lancaster County, Pennsylvania, Commissioners for Development and Revenue Sharing funds, and various corporate and private foundations. WITH A WIDE RANGE OF SUPPORT, OUR GOAL IS WELL WITHIN REACH.

The NAWCC Museum, Inc., stands ready to assist you with information about your timepieces, information, the irretrievable loss of which would be tragic. WITH YOUR HELP, OUR FUTURE IS BRIGHT. Please send your tax-deductible contributions now.

Thank you and best wishes.

Sincerely,

Bruce G. Shoemaker
Development Officer

Fig. 1

Photos courtesy
NAWCC Museum Collection.

Fig. 2

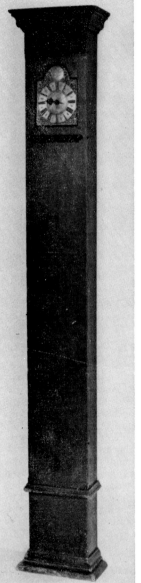

Fig. 3

JOHN FOSS/ SOMERSWORTH 30-HOUR TIMEPIECE CIRCA 1755

Probably the earliest piece in the 1984 summer exhibit at your NAWCC Museum is a timepiece made by John Foss who worked in Somersworth, NH. Little is known about the maker, and records show that several men by the name of John Foss lived in the area during that century. According to the *Genealogy of the Foss Family in America*, John the clockmaker was baptized in Rochester, NH, on September 18, 1732, and was the son of Joshua and Lydia (Rand) Foss, both of whom were born in Rye, NH. John Foss died in 1819 in his 88th year.

The movement (Figure 1) has a heavy plate frame which is cut out in the shape of an "I," with the train running straight up the center. It has a conventional recoil escapement with a seconds beat pendulum. The thick brass plates have very little finishing and the wheels are rather crudely crossed out. A spoke ratchet and rope pulley winding system is used. A single hand eliminated an extra wheel and pinion. The inner circle of the chapter ring (Figure 2) is marked off in quarter hours. Though minute hands were common on tall clocks after 1660, cheaper single-handed clocks continued to be made well into the 18th Century for the country trade. Though constructed as an inexpensive timepiece, this curious clock (Figure 3) with its simple pine case and interesting mouldings has more appeal today than many of its more sophisticated cousins.

Although the 1984 NAWCC Museum's summer exhibition closes on 31 October, many of the items will be placed on display at the New Hampshire Historical Society in Concord, NH, the end of November. We thank the following who made our exhibit possible: American Clock and Watch Museum, Bristol, CT; Herschel B. Burt; Currier Gallery of Art, Manchester, NH; Ward H. Francillon; A. E. Huson; Edward F. LaFond, Jr.; New Hampshire Antiquarian Society, Hopkinton, NH; New Hampshire Historical Society, Concord, NH; Old Sturbridge Village, Sturbridge, MA; Theo. R. Schwalm; Robert J. Shaull; and those who wish to remain anonymous. Finally, we are indebted to Charles S. Parsons who over the years assembled the largest known and most comprehensive collection of New Hampshire horology, studied it, recorded it, published it, and presented it to the New Hampshire Historical Society so that future generations could learn from it. Without his help and advice the NAWCC summer exhibition would not have been possible.

THE RECORDED WORD — CASSETTES NOW AVAILABLE (PART TWO)

Two more tapes have been added to the Lending Library collection. Both are from the 1983 Lancaster Seminar: "Lancaster, Pennsylvania, Mass-Produced Watches: Adams and Perry to the Hamilton Watch Co.," by Arthur Zimmerla; and, "Lancaster County (PA): Colonial Center of Clockmaking," by Stacy Wood. Order these as you would a book from the Lending Library.

RECENT DONATIONS TO THE NAWCC MUSEUM

Waterbury Clock Co. large pocket watch with alarm circa 1891; American Hard Rubber Co./New York "Watch Case Atomizer" with patent date of Aug. 1, 1899 (Steven Berger)

Miscellaneous clocks, watches, tools, etc. (August C. Bolino)

Orbital timepiece with case and display of polished aluminum and acrylic coating. Powered by a quartz movement. Model known as "Momentum." This particular item is from the first production run of 100 circa 1980. Invented and designed by the donor (Ronald L. Ferina)

Wm. L. Gilbert "Elberon" model calendar clock circa 1900 utilizing the W. R. McCabe non-perpetual calendar mechanism patent of 10 Nov 1896 (Edward and Gladys Greulich)

Mitterteich/Holland 7-piece set of "Porzellan" dishes with a picture of a different Dutch wall clock on each plate (Charles E. Johnson)

Battery-powered electronic clock beat setter; Erhard Jauch Uhrenfabrik/Germany timing unit; large platform escapement; and a mechanical counting device by an unknown manufacturer (Tom LaRose)

Hamilton Watch Co. "C" cell battery fit-up clock movement; Hamilton electric automobile clock; Hamilton Elinvar 992 3-piece demonstrator; Hamilton Allied Products Div. salesman's case with sample products in plexiglass cubes; and one each ladies' and men's wristwatch boxes (Robert E. Schafer)

Hammond Clock Co. desk calendar clock utilizing the Laurens Hammond patent of 2 July 1929 (Anonymous)

Silver watch fob with NAWCC logo (Chapter 76 — Timekeepers)

NEW ADDITIONS TO THE NAWCC LENDING LIBRARY

Not previously listed.

BOOKS

AUTHOR	TITLE	SOURCE
Auberson, Robert	*Les Cotes de l'Horlogerie Ancienne de la Renaissance a 1930 (1981)	Robert Auberson 84768
Daniels, Joseph W.	*How to Build 35 Great Clocks (1984) 2 copies	Stanley L. Kopia 14213
Earle, Alice M.	*Sun-Dials and Roses of Yesterday (1902-R)	Charles Rampe 7450
Ehrhardt, Sherry, and Peter Planes	*Vintage American & European Wrist Watch Price Guide (1984) 4 copies	Roy Ehrhardt 23096
Goaman, Murial	*English Clocks (1967)	
Holly, Forrest M.	For Generations to Come: The Life Story of Elias Ingraham (1975)	San Diego County Chapter 59
Rudolph, James S.	*Make Your Own Working Paper Clock (1983)	James W. Gibbs 79
Townsend, George E.	*American Pocket and Wrist Watch Balance Staff Interchangeability List (1984) 4 copies	RE 23096
Williams, Gary	*Designing and Building a Grandfather Clock (1980) 4 copies	Minnesota — Oscar T. Lang Memorial Chapter #20 in memory of Irving Moss, 36327 (2 copies); Tennessee Valley Chapter #42 in memory of William T. Heath, 31476 (2 copies)

Donald J. Summar, Librarian

EARLY GIANTS

ALBERT L. PARTRIDGE

by Charles S. Parsons

Albert L. Partridge died February 12, 1972. He will probably be best remembered for his long tenure as secretary-treasurer of the (Boston) Clock Club and his 27 contributions to the BULLETIN. He married his Maine academy sweetheart, Olive, who became his constant companion. Unfortunately they had no children, but their great love for each other was obvious. When Albert hesitated for a moment to recall a date, name, clock, or other fact, Olive was always prompt with the correct information. One wag said she knew more about clocks than he. This great companionship resulted in the many contributions that were made after thorough study. They were presented in an easily understood manner and sprinkled with his dry wit.

The April 1955 BULLETIN contains Albert's description of "The [Boston] Clock Club which was organized in Boston in 1934. The first meeting was held on January 13, 1934, and the last, April 6, 1940 — total number of meetings, 34. Following each meeting there were sent to members multigraphed bulletins of proceedings [written by A.L.P.] and of important material presented to the meeting, — a total of 209 pages. There was prepared and circulated an index covering all material except that appearing in the final five bulletins." Included in the bulletins are writings of some length on many horological subjects. It must be noted that at that time tape recorders were not available. In the first issue was a bibliography of clock books listing only five titles, showing that few books on clocks were readily available then.

I was greatly honored that Albert gave me his personal copy of the minutes which was interleafed with original letters that he later described: "After the Club closed up the shop, the Massachusetts State Library asked me for a full run of our publications and having furnished that I offered runs to other institutions, all offers being accepted with alacrity. I have cordial and complimentary acknowledgements from: Boston Atheneum, *Antiques*, Connecticut State Library, Yale University Library, University of Pennsylvania Library, American Antiquarian Society (Worcester, MA) which I submit, indicates that we were successful in getting our finished product into fairly fast company." From this the reader can appreciate his writing style and that copies are available at the named institutions.

Penrose Hoopes, the horological author, wrote to Lockwood Barr, another writer: "In my opinion there is no one in America who writes as well on clocks as Albert Partridge." The index of the BULLETIN, December 1959, No. 83, lists the great variety of subjects about which Albert wrote. He gave me his correspondence file and there were probably more letters regarding the origin of wooden movements than any other subject. After writing to various authorities in England and on the continent, he did not find the answer. His subjects were of a few clockmakers and of movements that interested him or on which there was nothing previously written.

Albert did not wish to hold office in the New England Chapter, although he was elected a trustee when his close friend Don Packard was its first President. He appears in a photo of Officers of the New England Chapter in the February 1951 BULLETIN.

Albert made three last requests of me. One was to write up the story of the first Terry patent about the equation clock. After he retired and before I did, we attempted to do something about the Terry patents. We originally hoped that Reg Morrell would contribute, but his duties at the Bristol Museum did not permit time to devote to that subject. When the Partridges went to Florida for the winter they had more time as I had not yet retired. He never did understand my explanation of the equation kidney cam which I thought was a very simple design.

A second request was to investigate the mysterious Willard shelf clocks at Winterthur and the Dedham Historical Society. I had all his correspondence with Professor Willis Milham, etc., photos supplied by Charles F. Montgomery at my request, and miscellaneous notes. There are parts missing on both examples. There is a table of figures on the inside of the back board. Some time ago I turned all of this over to Robert Cheney. Richard W.

Philbrick of Orleans, MA, believes he has deciphered the tables. He, Robert, and Herschel Burt have visited Dedham and taken the clock apart and taken photos. I have been very busy with other unfinished projects so have not participated. I shall try to encourage, if necessary, the completion of this study as Albert's wish. The third suggestion by Albert was a study of pocket sundials. I explained that this was a whole new field that I probably would never have time to investigate. Since then there has been something published.

I did work with Albert on the wooden pin wheel escapement clocks as written for the BULLETIN in 1962. The April 1960 issue has a story of the Manning clocks which was obviously Albert's writing. He insisted that it be submitted under my name and I put a final paragraph of explanation. He started to tear it up until I agreed to the use of my name. He used various ways to encourage me to write up my notes.

In addition to the BULLETIN, he wrote for the magazine *Antiques*, and *Old Time New England*, a publication of the Society for the Preservation of New England Antiquities. Herschel Burt disposed of most of his clocks after the Partridges moved to a retirement home in 1971. Previously they had given a number of clocks to the Shelburne Museum.

Albert had many other interests: lawn bowling; at one time a study of snails; and a study of Alaskan totem poles. In 1949 he wrote "An Early Gift of Land to Harvard College," which used his skills as a probate lawyer. In 1922 he wrote a "real property" handbook which he revised in 1960. He also contributed an article on "Simon Willard's Regulator Clocks," and several others.

The minutes of the October 1950 meeting at Old Sturbridge Village said: "The humor of Albert Partridge in his lecture 'What Is It?' had everyone convulsed with laughter."

This Renaissance man has indeed proven to be an Early Giant. The memory of his spirit and manner continues to inspire those of us who knew him. His work continues to benefit all horologists.

DATES TO REMEMBER

(Names in parenthesis are National Officers assigned to specific meetings.)

October 18-21, 1984 (Tom LaRose)
Mid-South Regional. Host — Dixie, #16. Co-hosts — Atlanta, #24; Tennessee Valley, #42; Rocket City Regulators, #61. Sheraton —Nashville Hotel, Nashville, TN

October 25-27, 1984
NAWCC Council Seminar, Sheraton Civic Center Plaza, Hartford, CT

November 2-3, 1984 (Tom LaRose)
Mid-Eastern Regional. Host — Carolina, #17. Co-hosts — Philadelphia, #1; Maryland, #11; Washington, DC, #12; Shenandoah Valley of Virginia, #32; Old Dominion, #34. Raddison Hotel, Charlotte, NC

November 9-11, 1984
M-K-O Regional. Host — Cherokee, #30. Co-hosts — Ozark, #57; Sunflower Clock Watchers, #63; Sooner Time Collectors, #74. Tulsa Marriott, Tulsa, OK

November 15-17, 1984 (Bernard Edwards)
Great Southwestern Regional. Host — Ark-La-Tex, #45. Co-hosts — Southwestern, #15; Arkansas Razorback, #62. Hilton Inn, Bossier City, LA

January 17-20, 1985 (Gene Bagwell)
Florida Mid-Winter Regional. Host — Florida Gold Coast, #60. Co-hosts — Florida Suntime, #19; Jean Ribault, #68; Florida White Sands, #96; Caloosa, #98; Palm Beaches of Florida, #99. Marriott's Resort & Beach Club, Ft. Lauderdale, FL

February 14-17, 1985
Pacific-Northwest Regional. Host — Puget Sound, #50. Co-hosts — Pacific-Northwest, #31; Inland Empire, #53. Tacoma Dome Convention Center, Tacoma, WA

February 28-March 2, 1985
Lone Star Regional. Host — Lone Star, #124. Co-hosts — Five State Collectors, #80; Rio Grande, #117. North Park Inn, Dallas, TX

March 8-10, 1985
North Coast Regional. Host — Lake Erie, #28. Co-hosts — Ohio Valley, #10; Firelands, #39. Holiday Inn, Strongsville, OH

March 28-31, 1985
Southern Regional. Host — Creole, #43. Co-hosts — Magnolia, #41; King Cotton, #48; Pelican State, #128. Landmark Motor Hotel, Metairie, LA

April 12-13, 1985
Southern Ohio Regional. Host — Buckeye, #23. Co-host — Central Ohio, #85. Drawbridge Motor Inn, Ft. Mitchell, KY

April 27-28, 1985
Greater New York Regional. Host — New York, #2. Co-host — American Watchmakers Institute, #102. Viscount International Hotel, New York, NY

May 17-19, 1985
Great Plains Regional. Host — Great Plains, #58. Co-host — Hawkeye, #91. Holiday Inn, Omaha, NE

May 24-25, 1985
St. Louis Regional. Host — St. Louis, MO, #14. Co-host — Little Egypt, #77. Concourse Hotel, St. Louis, MO

June 19-23, 1985
NAWCC National Convention. Georgia World Congress Center, Atlanta, GA

August 9-10, 1985
Rocky Mountain Regional. Host — Colorado Centennial, #100. Co-host — Colorado, #21. The Antlers Hotel, Colorado Springs, CO

August 23-25, 1985
Eastern States Regional. Host — Central New York, #55. Co-hosts — Western New York, #13; Toronto, #33. Sheraton Inn, Syracuse, Liverpool, NY

August 30-September 1, 1985
M-K-O Regional. Host — Ozark, #57. Co-hosts — Cherokee, #30; Sunflower Clock Watchers, #63. Howard Johnson's Motor Lodge, Springfield, MO

September 6-8, 1985
Great Lakes Regional. Host — Great Lakes, #6. Co-hosts — Saginaw Valley, #67; Western Michigan, #101. Hyatt Regency, Dearborn, MI
September 13-14, 1985
Kentucky Blue-Grass Regional. Host — Kentucky Blue-Grass, #35. Co-host Kentucky Floral Clock, #44. Holiday Inn South, Louisville, KY
September 26-28, 1985
Great Southwestern Regional. Host — Arkansas Razorback, #62. Co-hosts — Southwestern, #15; Ark-La-Tex, #45. Camelot Inn, Little Rock, AR
October 3-5, 1985
Mid-America Regional. Host — Indiana, #18. Co-host — George E. Lee Michiana, #26. Ft. Wayne Convention Center, Ft. Wayne, IN
October 18-19, 1985
NAWCC Council Seminar, Cosmopolitan Hotel, Portland, OR

NATIONAL CONVENTION DATES

Atlanta, GA — June 19-23, 1985   Anaheim, CA — June 10-14, 1987
Cleveland, OH — June 18-22, 1986   Orlando, FL — February 10-14, 1988
              Buffalo, NY — June 21-25, 1989

NAWCC COUNCIL SEMINAR DATES

Hartford, CT — October 25-27, 1984   Portland, OR — October 17-19, 1985
              Dearborn, MI — October 23-25, 1986

ALL REGIONAL MEETINGS ARE SCHEDULED AND LISTED HERE ONLY THROUGH THE CONVENTION COMMITTEE

Owen H. Burt, Chairman, 4438 Ramsgate Lane, Bloomfield Hills, MI 48013

NECROLOGY

Kirkwood B. Brown, #2966
S. Dennis, MA

Charles I. MacNeil, #74941
DeBary, FL

Floyd Campbell, #36457
Springfield, OH

C. G. Nelson, #45027
Walla Walla, WA

Jerry Chalcraft, #75818
Wilmette, IL

Burdet W. Oelschlegel, #14720
Terryville, CT

Andrew C. Chapin, #458
Sacramento, CA

Herbert D. Ralph, #52086
Grosse Pointe Farms, MI

William C. Ferguson, #61233
Montpelier, OH

George H. Reymond, #9287
Baton Rouge, LA

Hans Haas, #1299
San Francisco, CA

Cecil E. Sears, #6994
New Castle, IN

Forrest Handshaw, #73054
Clearwater, FL

Louie Fay Stamper, #45074
Long Beach, CA

Keith G. Hodgin, FNAWCC, #11533
Asheboro, NC

Dean R. VanAusdall, #27550
Northridge, CA

Vern L. Hursey, #60715
Cromwell, IN

Wells C. Woodard, Sr., #22085
Morrisville, VT

Willard LeCroy, #40590
San Jose, CA

Burley M. Woodlief, #73166
Richmond, VA

Thomas H. Zinn, #15791
Columbus, OH

Research Activities and News

Snowden Taylor, Research Committee Chairman,
318 Western Highway, Tappan, NY 10983

DR. AMOS COLLINS, CLOCKMAKER

by Jacque Houser

Probate papers, recently brought to our attention by Sara Steiner of Rhode Island, reveal additional details of a relatively obscure Rhode Island clockmaker. The man was Dr. Amos Collins of Cranston, RI, whose estate was probated in 1851. The inventory of the estate, briefly mentioned in this section of the December, 1983, issue of the BULLETIN, has been transcribed and is now available on loan from the libraries of NAWCC and AC&WM.

Some of the items inventoried suggest that Dr. Collins was engaged in some phase of the clock business; probably producing shelf clocks with purchased brass movements installed in cases made in his own shop.

Principal support for this hypothesis is found in the following three listings from the first page of the inventory: 12 Brass clocks $1.00 each, 12.00; Lumber for clock cases in shop chamber, 8.00; Old iron, clock weights, & old boxes in shop chamber, 2.50.

If we assume that the brass clocks were actually brass movements — the assigned value substantiates this — we see that he could have been putting movements in cases made in his shop. The list of tools found in the two, or possibly three, shops contains the following items which could be used for case making: Cutting machine at Fiskville factory, 12.00; 2 small turning lathes at $10 each, 20.00; 1 turning engine in upper mill, 15.00; Work bench in lower mill, 2.00; Iron vice in lower mill, 1.00.

The only other clock related items found in the inventory are three brass clocks valued at $5.00 (erroneously given as $3.00 in the December BULLETIN), included in the furnishings of Dr. Collins' home.

Very little was found in the inventory that would be connected to his medical practice. Twenty medical books and a case of medicine drawers are self evident. Some of the furniture may have been used in his office but none was identified as being used for that purpose. The total value of the estate was stated to be about $450.00 of which $174.70 consisted of notes owed the Doctor by ten persons. Unfortunately we find no clues that might tie these debts to Dr. Collins' clock business. Nevertheless, we feel that the contents of the inventory establish without question that Dr. Collins was in the clock business and that he was probably assembling clocks from purchased movements and self-made cases. The output of his operation must depend upon further research for definition.

(Chairman's notes: Just to prove that research is a controversial business, and that members of the Research Committee do not always agree with each other, the Chairman interprets the data on the Dr. Collins operation as suggesting that he *did* make brass movements as well as cases, the entire operation having ended some years prior to the 1851 probate. Does any member have an Amos Collins or Collins & Co. Rhode Island clock to report?)

THE FEDERAL CLOCK SHOP DISCOVERED

by Jacque Houser

An extensive study of old journals which have recently become the property of the American Clock and Watch Museum is revealing much previously unknown information about our horological heritage. One of these journals appears to be an account book of the Federal Clock Shop of Waterbury, CT. The proprietors of the Clock Shop are identified by two entries in the journal. The first, on page 2, states:

Wm. K. Lamson; Mark Leavenworth; Anson Sperry; Clockmakers, Waterbury, CT, New Haven County.

The last page in the journal carries the following note:

Wm. K. Lamson; Mark Leavenworth; Anson Sperry; Proprietors of the Federal Clock Shop in Waterbury.

The journal presents an accounting of the transactions of Lamson, Leavenworth, and Sperry from late 1810 until mid 1813, thus extending the recorded details of Mark Leavenworth's activities four years earlier than the earliest date in his previously known journals.[1]

Chris Bailey, in an article in the BULLETIN, has shown that these three men were in a partnership known as Lamson, Sperry & Co. during the greatest portion of this period.[2] Leavenworth joined Wm. K. Lamson and Anson Sperry, operating as Lamson and Sperry, in June of 1811 at which time the name of the partnership was changed to Lamson, Sperry & Co. Leavenworth bought out his partners about March 28, 1814. From these new accounts we conclude that the partnership was identified as Lamson, Sperry, & Co., but that the shop itself was known as the Federal Clock Shop.

Although the partnership was made up of Lamson, Leavenworth, and Sperry all clock sales were credited to Sperry and Lamson or Lamson and Leavenworth. (Sometimes the order of the names was reversed but never was the pairing changed.) Two lists of sales are maintained in the journal. The first is headed "May 31, 1811, Memorandum of Sperry and Lamson Clocks," and covers the period from that date to February 2, 1813. The second is headed "Waterbury June 8, 1811, Memorandum of Lamson & Leavenworth Clocks," and covers a period from that date through May 30, 1812. (Chairman's note: All of the "clocks" mentioned in this document are 30-hr. wooden tall clock movements. "DM" means "Day of the Month.") The existence of the two separate entities within the partnership is confirmed by many other entries in the journal. For example:

May 29, 1811 Dr
Lamson & Leavenworth to parts borrowed
pendulum balls   57
bob screws   20
wait tops   63
bel shafts   18
July 9, 1811
Robert Pope, 48 DM Clocks & 18 Plane of
Lamson, Sperry & Co.   66
and 3 D.M. 3 plane Borrowed of S & Lamson
Sept 18, 1811
Leavenworth & Lamson borrowed of the Co., 5 DM Clocks for Smith — 20th Sept borrowed of the Company 15 Plain Clocks for the Kassons — parts were furnished with the above 20 clocks.

And finally:

Sept 24, 1811
Reckoned all the Clocks borrowed or Lent and finds due the Company from Leavenworth & Lamson 5 DMonth & 14 Plain Clocks
Leavenworth & Lamson Cr
By 1 DM Clock charged to A Austin, 24th Sept
By 50 Month Clocks for Parker
do 12 Equally assorted for Aaron Bronson.

Other examples could be cited, but the point has been demonstrated that at least for bookkeeping purposes there were two divisions in the Company.

There is nothing in the journal to indicate the date of the termination or dissolution of the Company, which, as mentioned earlier, probably took place in late March of 1814 when Leavenworth bought out his partners. Since this newly discovered journal has no entries later than 1813 we suspect that there is another journal, as yet undiscovered, which contains additional information of the activities of the Company. This hypothesis finds further support in the lists of clocks sold. The Sperry and Lamson list ends February 2, 1813, while the Lamson & Leavenworth list ends May 30, 1812. No blank pages are present in the book and the different dates for ending the lists reinforces the belief that the record was continued in another book.

Sales of clocks, during the period for which we have records, were quite impressive. During the slightly more than twenty-one months documented, 6765 clocks were delivered, which reduces to about 322 clocks per month. Unfortunately, there is little in the account book that can be used to define the work force of the enterprise. Only four entries, for four men totaling $26.72, can be found which might be construed to be for clock labor. This reduces to about 30 days at the then current wages.

The absence of a large number of accounts for payments to a labor force suggests that Mark Leavenworth and Anson Sperry were the principal source of shop labor. Salaries paid were given for only one worker. Jude Clark received $1.00 per day on one job and 83⅓ cents per day for another. The work done was not identified. We only assume that it was clock related. During the twenty-one-month period under study, Lamson & Leavenworth were credited with 3003 clocks while Lamson & Sperry were credited with 3753. Nine of the total delivered were credited to neither of the two divisions — presumably credited directly to the Company.

We note that the Company had business relationships with many of the prominant personages in the early Connecticut clock industry. We find records indicating that the Company borrowed 38 pair of cannisters (weight cans) from Edward Porter and returned the loan seven months later. Edward Porter, in turn, received pendulum rods, bell shafts, and bob screws, by loan or direct sale, from the Company. In early June of 1812, Edward Porter received 3 clocks on the Sperry & Lamson account. On January 19, 1813, L. Porter (presumed to be Levi) received a single clock on the Sperry & Lamson account. Edward and Levi Porter were the persons who negotiated the unprecedented contract with Eli Terry for 4000 30-hour wood pull-up movements to be delivered by Terry in three years.[3] Lemuel Harrison & Co., early clock manufacturer who employed Ephraim Downs, was indebted to the Company for #1 & #4 wire and pendulum rods by an entry dated August 24, 1812. Other entries, relating Lemuel Harrison & Co. to the Company are found throughout the journal. An early entry states that Mr. Zenas Cook began to keep horses for Porter and Clark. A Daniel Clark received 50 clocks from the Company in July of 1811. Daniel Clark, Zenas Cook, and William Porter formed a partnership January 1, 1811, with Lemuel Harrison to form Lemuel Harrison & Co.[4] The clocks delivered to Daniel Clark were probably for Lemuel Harrison & Co. not for the personal use of Daniel Clark.

This latest microfilm received by the Research Committee from the American Clock and Watch Museum contains, in addition to the Federal Clock Shop records, journals of Mark Leavenworth (1831-1833), Elisha Manross, David Pritchard, and H. Welton & Co. These records will be transcribed, where necessary, and indexed and made available on loan at the NAWCC and AC&WM libraries for the convenience of horological history buffs.

NOTES

1. The Mark Leavenworth journals have been transcribed and indexed and will be available on loan from the NAWCC and AC&WM libraries.

2. Chris H. Bailey, "Mr. Terry's Waterbury Competitors," NAWCC BULLETIN, Vol. XXI, No. 3, June, 1979.

3. Virginia and Howard Sloane, "4000 Clocks, The Story of Eli Terry and His Mysterious Financiers," NAWCC BULLETIN, Vol. XXII, No. 1, February, 1980.

4. Chris H. Bailey, *Two Hundred Years of American Clocks and Watches*, Prentice Hall, Inc., page 107.

DOCUMENT TRANSCRIPTION

The probate records of Northrop & Smith (1836 — bankruptcy) and Dr. Amos Collins (1851 — death) have been transcribed and filed with the NAWCC Research Library, Columbia, PA, and the American Clock and Watch Museum, Bristol, CT.

LABEL PRINTER PROJECT

The first tangible product of this project has now appeared: "Printers of Hartford 1825 thru 1860," by D. R. Slaght. Don Slaght has extracted all of the printers from the Hartford, CT, City Directories of the above dates, and produced this 83-page document. It is available at cost from NAWCC Headquarters, Columbia, PA. Thanks, Don, for this major effort.

BULLETIN SUPPLEMENT NO. 14 — AMERICAN WATCHMAKING

The Committee notes with great pleasure the publication of "American Watchmaking: A Technical History of the American Watch Industry, 1850-1930," by Michael C. Harrold. Committee Member Eugene Fuller "shepherded" this effort from the start, and wrote the Foreword. The Committee also sponsored this publication in a small way by covering the costs of preparing some of the tables and charts. Thanks, Mike Harrold, for this fine book, and thanks Gene Fuller, for your help.

MORE ON THE DEMILT FAMILY

Ted Crom, in this column in the April 1984 BULLETIN, noted that Elizabeth Demilt was the wife of watchshop proprietor Samuel Demilt. The Chairman inserted a note that the inventory of the estate of Sarah Demilt seemed to show that *she* was the wife of Samuel. It turns out that we were both wrong!

Recently, the Chairman visited Prof. Leo Hershkowitz of our "Queens College Project." Leo suggested that we look up the Demilt wills, available in the Queens College, NY, Historical Documents Collection. In a brief search, we were not able to identify Isaac or Thomas Demilt, but we were able to establish that Benjamin, Samuel, Phebe, Sarah, and Elizabeth Demilt were all children of Peter Demilt. It appeared that none of the children married except Benjamin. Hence both Elizabeth and Sarah were sisters of Samuel, living at Samuel's 7 Rutgers Place home at the time of his death or shortly thereafter. This was a wealthy family. Old Peter must have been very successful in the tailor business!

DOCUMENTS FROM THE SUPREME COURT, CITY AND COUNTY OF NEW YORK

At the invitation of Prof. Leo Hershkowitz (see above), the Chairman spent half a day at the Hall of Records in New York City where a room full of documents from the Supreme Court, City and County of New York, were being culled from the permanent records. These documents are not the full records of the court cases involved, but are court orders and related affidavits, depositions, etc. Frequently the documents in the file give little or no clue to the nature of the court case, but in some, more information is revealed. Rarely is one able to determine the ultimate disposition of the case. Altogether, with Leo's help, the Chairman collected the documents pertaining to ten cases involving clock companies or personalities. All of these will ultimately be deposited in the NAWCC Research Library, Columbia, PA.

Augustus S. Jerome vs. William S. Corwin, 1872-74. Little can be learned from these documents other than the fact that this son of Chauncey Jerome was involved in this suit during these dates.

The Ansonia Brass and Copper Company vs. The National Musical Instrument Manufacturing Co., 1880-1881, and *In the Matter of The Application of the Ansonia Brass & Copper Company, to continue its lien in respect of a public improvement, being the New Armory Building for the Second Battalion of Naval Militia . . ., 1906.* In neither of these cases is there any evidence that the Ansonia Brass & Copper Co., "a corporation existing under the laws of the State of Connecticut," is a clock company. Both cases involve debts due the Company, and in the 1906 case the debt involves "Cold Rolled Copper for use on roof." In 1880, the Company is described as "having a place of business in the City and County of New York," and in 1906 "has its principal place of business within the State of New York, at No. 99 John Street, in the Borough of Manhattan, City of New York." In 1880, Alfred A. Cowles is identified as the Secretary of the Company, and in 1906, Russell A. Cowles is identified as Treasurer.

The Ansonia Clock Company vs. Charles McCulloch Beecher, Frank R. Johnson, Walter S. Baillie and Henry Paine Bartlett, 1892-1893. Little can be learned from the documents other than that the Ansonia Clock Co. brought a suit during the above dates. Note that the dates fall between those of the two Ansonia Brass & Copper Co. cases, so it would appear that both companies were active at the same time.

American Watchman's Time Detector Company vs. William F. Pettes, Asa S. Randall, and the New York Telephone Company, 1904. The documents pertaining to this case actually provide some material of direct horological interest. One of the documents presented to the court is a list of "Findings of Fact," prepared by the plaintiff's attorneys. In the margin, next to each "finding," is written in longhand either "Found" or "Not found," presumably by the judge. Quoted below are the items deemed "Found" by the judge, supplemented occasionally by material (in parentheses) extracted from another document, "Brief on Behalf of the Plaintiff:"

On or about March 31, 1882, letters patent were issued to J. A. Lannert and George F. Ranson [sic — Ransom] for a form of electrical clock, to which was given the name American Watchman's Time Detector. (. . . the object of which was to register upon a paper dial upon a central clock by an electrical connection, the movements of watchmen from separate stations.)

About the year 1883 the patent so issued passed into the hands of the Cleveland Electrical Manufacturing Company of Cleveland, Ohio, which thereafter continued to manufacture American Watchman's Time Detectors until the year 1900.

In 1900 the Cleveland Electrical Manufacturing Company was succeeded in business by the American Watchman's Time Detector Company of Ohio.

The letters patent covering the American Watchman's Time Detector expired in the year 1899.

From the year 1883 to the year 1891 the American Watchman's Time Detectors manufactured by the Cleveland Electrical Manufacturing Company were sold in the City of New York and in the adjoining territory, with the consent of the Cleveland Electrical Manufacturing Company, only by one Jamin S. Morse.

In the year 1891 Morse organized the American Watchman's Time Detectors Company under the laws of New Jersey, and turned his business over to it.

Following its organization, the American Watchman's Time Detector Company of New Jersey bought American Watchman's Time Detectors from the Cleveland Electrical Manufacturing Company, and resold them in the City of New York and adjoining territory.

In the year 1899 the plaintiff [American Watchman's Time Detector Company] was organized under the laws of the State of New York, by the same persons who controlled the American Watchman's Time Detector Company, of New Jersey, and succeeded to all the property and business of the latter corporation. (Subsequently to its organization, the American Watchman's Time Detector Company of New York manufactured time detectors and other electrical devices in addition to purchasing and selling the Cleveland article.)

In the year 1901 the defendant William F. Pettes, who had been in the employment of J. S. Morse and of his successors, left that employment, and with the defendant Asa S. Randall as partner went into the business among other things of selling, installing and repairing American Watchman's Time Detectors.

The defendants Pettes and Randall carried on their business as a partnership under the firm name 'Pettes & Randall.'

The defendants Pettes and Randall caused the names 'American Watchman's Clock Company' and 'American Watchman's Clock Company, Supply Department' to be inserted in the telephone directory of defendant the New York Telephone Company immediately preceding the name of the plaintiff, and opposite thereto they caused to be placed the telephone number of their firm of Pettes & Randall.

Before the defendants Pettes and Randall commenced business the plaintiff and its predecessor, the American Watchman's Time Detector Company of New Jersey, had frequently been spoken of as the 'American Watchman's Clock Company.'

The name 'American Watchman's Clock Company' was placed by the defendants Pettes and Randall in the telephone directory immediately preceding the name of the plaintiff for the purpose of misleading customers who intended to deal with the plaintiff into dealing with the defendants Pettes and Randall.

That was apparently the history and the essence of the case as "found" by the judge. Nevertheless, in the listing of "Conclusions of Law" which followed the "Findings of Fact," the words "Not found" are entered beside each one! Hence it is doubtful that the American Watchman's Time Detector Company of New York won this case.

As a footnote, it is of interest that in the Brief, cited above, a case *Roy Watch Case Company v. Camm — Roy Watch Case Co.*, 28 Misc., 45-48, is referred to. Camm — Roy Watch Case Co. lost that case.

In a future BULLETIN, in this column, the Chairman will describe the remainder of these court cases.

REQUESTS FOR ASSISTANCE:

JAMES W. KRAUSE REQUEST: JACQUES CLOCK CO. AND ASSOCIATED COMPANIES

"I am researching the Jacques Clock Co. and its associated co.'s of Bano & Dotter (Limited) and George Borgfeldt & Co. located in the NY area 1880-1930. While they dealt in all types of clocks I am especially interested in the grandfather clocks marketed under the Jacques name as well as Elite, Excelsior, and Monastery. Of particular interest is the 13-tube Jacques grandfather marketed after 1910. Anyone with any of these clocks providing information will be given credit or can remain anonymous if preferred. These clocks are quite unique and are covered by many patents making them a valuable link to the horological past. Please reply with any information you may have to: JAMES W. KRAUSE, 16382 MARUFFA CIRCLE, HUNTINGTON BEACH, CA 92649."

JOHN YOUNG REQUEST: WILTSHIRE, ENGLAND, CLOCKMAKERS

"I am writing a book on the clockmakers of Wiltshire, England. Many people from this county emigrated to the States in the early 19th Century often taking with them this most treasured possession, the clock. Many clocks have also been exported from the county in more recent years.

"I would very much like to hear from anybody who has a Wiltshire clock, or who thinks he may have, giving the name of the maker, the place where it was made, and a brief description of the clock. I will supply any details which I can in return.

Please reply to: JOHN YOUNG, 24 LITTLE PARKS, HOLT, NR TROW-BRIDGE, WILTSHIRE, BA14 6QR, ENGLAND."

WARD FRANCILLON REQUEST: ELI TERRY LABELED INSIDE-OUTSIDE ESCAPE PILLAR & SCROLL CLOCKS

"In the process of helping the Connecticut Historical Society assemble pre-standard Pillar & Scroll clocks and all the known 'box clocks' for the exhibit which supports the 5th Annual NAWCC Seminar, it has been noted just how few examples are known, and that fewer still are in complete or near-original condition. This particular exhibit opportunity is past, or passing, but the need to document, measure, and photograph good examples is still present and represents a real shortfall.

"We hope this Seminar and the four-month CHS exhibit that opens in October in Hartford will be the most comprehensive viewing and discussion of these landmark specimens to date. The write-ups and articles to follow will be that much better with the addition of data from any of these scarce specimens that can be located.

"If you have, or know the whereabouts of, additional examples of the Eli Terry Inside-Outside Escape Pillar & Scroll (see Figures 1-3), your assistance is sought for permission to examine and photograph such specimens for historical documentation. I would appreciate your help and can assure you that your wishes as to identification of location and ownership will be fully respected. Please reply to: WARD FRANCILLON, 24482 SPARTAN, MISSION VIEJO, CA 92691."

Fig. 1 View of front plate of movement mounted in P & S case of an Eli Terry Inside-Outside Escape clock. Note the escape wheel bridge is fastened to the movement front plate. (Photos courtesy of a private collection)

Fig. 3 View of the P & S label "PAT-ENT," with the words "INVENTED / MADE and SOLD by /ELI TERRY, / PLYMOUTH" in the oval. It is believed that all inside-outside movement clocks have the word "INVENTED" on the label. Your comments, please.

Fig. 2 View of the P & S backboard showing the three wood studs permanently set in the backboard to which the movement is fastened and secured by pins in the usual manner.

THE NAWCC MUSEUM'S FIFTH SILENT AUCTION OF BOOKS

The fifth silent auction of horological books and periodicals declared redundant by the NAWCC Museum Library Committee was announced in the September 1984 issue of the NAWCC MART. In accordance with NAWCC Museum Bylaws, items will be sold as individual items or lots to the highest bidder. All bidders must be members of NAWCC.

Outstanding items in this auction include various editions of F. J. Britten's *Old Clocks and Watches and Their Makers* (at reduced minimum bids); Chapuis & Droz, *Les Automates* (1949); Chapuis & Gelis, *Le Monde des Automates* (1928), two volumes, complete; many bound volumes of the B.H.I.'s *Horological Journal;* many volumes of *Antiquarian Horology* (at reduced minimum bids); NAWCC BULLETIN Reprints, Supplements, and loose copies of many issues; two lots of runs of the NAWCC MART; bound volumes and loose issues by year of the English, French, and German editions of *Swiss Watch & Jewelry Journal*; and Charles W. Moore's *Timing a Century: History of the Waltham Watch Company* (1945).

The silent auction includes 160 lots of books, 168 lots of periodicals (not counting NAWCC items), and 73 lots of reprinted trade catalogs. Many books and periodicals left over from previous silent auctions, and all reprinted trade catalogs, will be offered with NO MINIMUM BID! Many other books and periodicals from previous silent auctions are offered at much reduced minimum bids.

Catalogs of the silent auction are available to members of NAWCC by sending a self-addressed stamped envelope (4.1" x 9.5" size), with 37¢ in stamps affixed, to: NAWCC BOOK AUCTION, Box 33, Columbia, PA 17512. Overseas membe.s should use International Postal Orders for two ounces postage. Bid sheets must be returned to the NAWCC Museum by February 1, 1985.

Donald J. Summar, Librarian

VOX TEMPORIS

ADDITIONAL ADDENDUM TO BUCKEYE HOROLOGY

Under Fairfield County only three clockmakers named Sturgeon were listed. In the February, 1984, *THE MAGAZINE ANTIQUES*, there is an article, "Ohio Furniture 1788-1888," by E. Jane Connell, Assistant Curator, Columbus Museum of Art, and Charles R. Mullen, Guest Curator. In Harrison no clockmaker was really established.

These authors state that Caleb Hibbard, Jr., moved from Chester County, Pennsylvania, to Harrison County, Ohio, where he continued to make clocks. Figure 1 of their article is a photograph of a Hibbard clock and this descriptive information:

> Tall-case clock made by Caleb Hibbard, Jr. (1781-1835), Harrison County, after 1818. Inscribed "Caleb Hibbard / Harrison C / Ohio" on the dial. Cherry; height 98, width 18¾, depth 10¾ inches.

Caleb Hibbard was the third generation of Quaker clockmakers to work in Willistown T o w n s h i p, Chester County, Pennsylvania. In 1818, he migrated to Ohio and settled near the border of Harrison and Tuscarawas counties. Little is known about his career in Ohio except that in 1832 he lived briefly in Barnesville where he set up a silversmithing shop. It had been thought that he did not continue to make clocks in Ohio, but this signed example suggests otherwise.

James W. Gibbs, Ph.D.
5450 Wissahickon Ave.
Philadelphia, PA 19144

* * *

UNUSUAL STREET CLOCK

The photograph is of a street clock which I designed and assembled and have operating on the front lawn of my home. It took me about six years to gather enough pieces to put it together and get it operating properly, but it was a satisfying project and has created considerable interest in our town and surrounding areas. Very few of our residents had ever seen a clock of this type or size.

The 9' tall clock is finished in bronze and is equipped with 15" lighted dials and a copper and brass weather vane top finial. The base and stand were part of an old traffic light. The clock hands are activated through magnetic movements by 6V, DC impulses transmitted and controlled by an IBM International Master Clock, model #13-7, with Invar pendulum, ca. 1920. The movements are from an Electrique Brille from a government office in Dunlop, France. The clock is equipped with correction features to keep it synchronized with WWV, coordinated universal time signal, and it is accurate within five to ten seconds per week.

Harold M. Yoakum
411 Downing Rd.
P.O. Box 34
Scott City, KS 67871

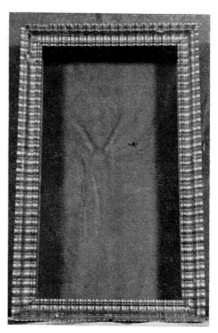

Fig. 2 Close-up view of the frame that holds the barometer scale which shows the detail of the ripple.

A RARE CLOCK BY NOAH POMEROY

The photographs show a very rare A m e r i c a n combination barometer, thermometer, and clock manufactured by Noah Pomeroy, ca. 1850. The clock is 49″ high and 13¾″ at its widest point. Not easily visible in the picture is the fact that this clock is fully rippled. Ripple moulding runs the entire length of the sides, forms the frames for the barometer and thermometer, and forms the frame around the dial. The drop portion of the clock, which contains the barometer and thermometer, is OG in contour and made with a beautiful flame mahogany veneer. This type of American barometer, thermometer rippled wall clock appears to be very rare.

The barometer is signed Woodroffe and the name and scales are printed on paper labels. The thermometer has interesting temperature highlights: freezing at 32°, temperate at 55° (to me that's cold or at least cool), sun heat at 76°, blood heat at 98°, and fever heat at 112°.

Fig. 1 Front view of the ripple barometer thermometer wall clock with movement by Noah Pomeroy. The dial has been cut out to show the balance wheel.

Fig. 3 Front view of the barometer label made of paper. Underneath is another complete paper label.

Noah Pomeroy, but rather his movements were purchased and utilized by whomever manufactured and sold it. There is even a remote possibility that the case and barometer were made up in England and the movements installed there. But, I think more likely it is an American product. It would be good to find who 'Woodroffe' was.

"Noah Pomeroy, son of Hiram and Ruby (Parsons) Pomeroy was born at Somers, CT, December 29, 1819. He came to Bristol in the mid-1840's and became involved in the clock business.

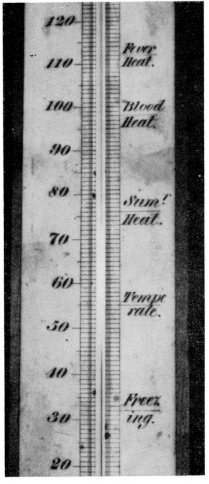

The movement is an 8-day marine type. Under the balance wheel is the signature, N. Pomeroy / Bristol CT U.S. This signature suggests that the clock may have been made for the export market as it clearly states U.S.

This clock, which is all original, was a joy to recondition. The size and fragility of the clock would tend to cause it to be easily damaged. Thankfully this example made it through the rigors of the past 130 years. I would be most interested in hearing from other members who own examples of this clock or any others of similar type.

Thomas Grimshaw
470 Riverside Dr.
Cheshire, CT 06410

(Editor's note: Chris Bailey of the American Clock & Watch Museum, Bristol, CT, adds these comments.)
"I doubt this barometer was sold by

Fig. 4 Front view of the temperature scale. Like the barometer scale it is made of paper and has an identical label underneath.

Fig. 5 Front view of the 8-day marine movement by Noah Pomeroy.

Fig. 6 Close-up view of the signature of N. Pomeroy below the balance wheel.

In 1849 he purchased the Chauncey Ives factory on Federal Street which he ran, sometimes in partnership with others, until selling out to Hiram Thompson in 1878. Though you occasionally see clocks l a b e l l e d Noah Pomeroy or Pomeroy & Parker, these are unusual. However, he sold a lot of movements, particularly 'marine' or balance escapement movements to the trade. So, when one sees the name Noah Pomeroy on the movement of a clock, it is often a clock that was cased up and marketed by another firm rather than Pomeroy.

"After selling out his business in 1878, Noah moved to Hartford, CT. He died while on a trip to San Francisco, CA, June 9, 1896."

(Editor's note: Your NAWCC Museum has a clock like this one. It is an N. Pomeroy marine-lever 8-day timepiece with "No. 376" stamped on the movement. The case is the same with the barometer and thermometer, but the label is marked, "Woodroffe and Wybred" instead of just "Woodroffe." Also, "Baltimore" is marked at the bottom of the barometer label. Examine this interesting clock on your next Museum visit.)

* * *

HOROLOGY, HORRIFYING

In an attempt to better our organization's public image, I would like to exhort, with tongue in cheek, the members of our prestigious NAWCC to discover a more dignified appelation for our communal pursuit that we now call "horology." Despite the honorable and ancient origin of the word, horology, to many, seems a little tacky. To laymen, discovering that we claim to be horologists or are pursuing horology, the connotation is that we, in however respectable manner, have something to do with trolleps and tarts, chippies and floozies. The phonetic resemblance is i n e s c a p a b l e enough that, to a person whose thinking is skewed to the lewd, our avocation borders on the bawdy.

From the thousands of our members, surely there could come a winning suggestion for a word that would describe or designate our hobby and convey to the public a sense of esteem for our group devoid of any tattyness. Personally, I would rather be known as a chronographer than as a horologist.

B. E. Johnson
1675 N.W. 70th Ave.
Ankeny, IA 50021

*

For some time I have reflected upon the descriptive title "antiquarian horologist," which seems clumsy and overly long, and have tried to think up some term which would be brief, unique, and acceptable to the old clock- and watch-collecting fraternity — something that could be a coined word like "numismatist" for coin collectors, "philatelist" for stamp collectors, or "deltiologist" for postcard collectors, etc.

My best idea so far would be the word "ALTUHRIST" from the German words for "old" and "clock." Derived words could be: "ALTUHRISM" — the collecting of old clocks; "ALTUHRIC" — referring to collecting.

If this idea makes sense to you, perhaps there could be a contest for a better word, making use of the total knowledge of NAWCC, and perhaps finding another, more euphonious and etymologically correct term to be adopted by the Association.

Dr. Francis J. Kearley, Jr.
4121 Ursuline Dr.
Mobile, AL 36608

* * *

STOLEN CLOCK

It is a large wall clock with an oak case approximately 56" long made by Seth Thomas Clock Co., Circa 1925.

The clock is equipped with an 8-day weight-powered movement with two cut glass jars in its pendulum. Each jar contains approximately 6 pounds of mercury. It has a Montgomery dial. The movement is a dead-beat with a sweepsecond hand (red). I would appreciate members' cooperation in trying to locate this clock. The identification number 1193 is stamped inside the clock case.

Please send any information to one of these offices:

Bill Boatman
Santa Fe Police Department
A.T. & S.F. Railway Co.
202 South Cleveland Ave.
Waynoka, OK 73860
Phone (405) 824-9551

Neil Crow
General Watch Inspector
Santa Fe Motive Power Bldg.
1001 N.E. Atchison
Topeka, KS 66616
Phone (913) 295-5799

Major County Sheriff
Fairview, OK 73737
Phone (405) 227-4471

David Nicholson (NAWCC #075662)
Santa Fe Local Time Inspector
115 W. Broadway, Room 7
Enid, OK 73701

THE ANSWER BOX

managed for the members of the NAWCC
by
John Cammarata
at the old stand of Messrs. Benis, Fried, and Edwards
WARRANTED IF WELL USED

This department is staffed with volunteers who answer horological questions from NAWCC members. The responders are authorities in various fields, and will try to provide any information requested on particular clocks or watches. **Absolutely no appraisals will be made!**

Address your query to The Answer Box, John Cammarata, 30 Lilac Drive, Syosset, NY 11791.

Put **only one query per letter** since each letter is redirected to the appropriate horological specialist. **Include your membership number with each request.**

Include a **self-addressed, stamped envelope with your letter** so that you may receive a personal reply. Non U.S. residents please include an International Reply Coupon. This stamp is your only service charge.

Supply as many descriptive details as possible. See "Points to Consider When Describing Watches or Clocks." Strive for legibility and clarity in your letter.

Send clear photos whenever possible. Black and white pictures are much preferred for reproduction in the BULLETIN. When photos are unavailable, good sketches are very helpful. Note: the pictures that are sent cannot be returned; surely the cost of a duplicate photo is less than the value of the information obtained.

(Answer Box material published in the BULLETIN is selected on the basis of general interest and information content. Only a small fraction of queries answered reach the BULLETIN pages. Ed.)

*

POINTS TO CONSIDER WHEN DESCRIBING

WATCHES	or	CLOCKS
size and jeweling plate structure method of winding serial number identifying markings	movement	type of layout material of construction power source identifying markings
type hairspring characteristics balance wheel structure	escapement	type pendulum characteristics provision for regulation
material size and type identifying marks	case	size and type primary and secondary materials style features
material and finish type of numerals secondary bits	dial	material and finish size, shape and layout type of numerals
material decorative characteristics method of setting	hands	material decorative characteristics method of setting
type of repetition automation alarm	strike	striking pattern bell or gong alarm

These points are intended only to stimulate logical and comprehensive descriptions of horologiana. Do not limit your description to the above factors. If there are others that you consider important, include them also.

STATUE OF LIBERTY?

From: Rick Newman, Box 141, S. Fallsburg, NY 12779

Between 1890 and 1920 American clock manufacturers produced many statue clocks, with, in my opinion, Ansonia and New Haven producing the nicest ones. The French also produced clocks of this type, although usually with marble bases, and larger.

With all of this, I have not seen America's most famous statue, the Statue of Liberty, pictured in any of my clock books. If you know of such a clock ever being produced I would appreciate any information or reference such as maker, date of manufacture, size, etc., so I could advertise to obtain such a clock.

I have a French statue clock which appears to be the Statue of Liberty sitting down. It is 22" H, on a marble base with clock; she has flowing robes, the torch in hand, and a crown (without the points, which stick out on the real statue). Instead of holding a tablet her other hand is under her chin.

While I have never given it any previous thought, you are absolutely right that the Statue of Liberty has never been reproduced for use with a clock by either American or French clock manufacturers. There is a cheap, white-metal novelty reproduction of the SOL that I once saw, with weight in its base and jewel bar soldered to where the torch is, sporting a Junghans movement, but somehow it didn't look right to me even though it was a well-done conversion and the clock was running.

Of course the statue is a sentimental symbol to hundreds of thousands of immigrants and it's very possible that many of these people would take offense at any attempt to degrade its significance by associating it with a clock, particularly a swinging clock; and when you think about it, perhaps no manufacturer wanted to subject himself to possible negative criticism. The one you describe, while close, is not actually the Statue of Liberty.

(Charles Terwilliger)

* * *

REPEATER WATCH

From: An anonymous member.

I would appreciate all the information available on the watch described here. An 18S, 18K, hunting case, unsigned dial, Roman numerals, gold spade hands, gold seconds hand, stem wind, lever set, 17J, cut balance, movement is not signed, covered with glass. Over the glass there is a highly polished gold cuvette with the following on it: Remontoir / Ancre / Ligne, droite spiral Breguet / CHaton / Repetition / A Quarts /Levees Visibles / N. 152821. (That number and Karat.)

Markings 0.750 are inside the case, on both covers, and on inside gold cuvette. The layout of movement is identical to the movement in the June 1983 BULLETIN, p. 275, Fig. 4B E. Bourquin minute repeater, except that it has fewer jewels.

When and where was the watch made? How m a n y repeaters were made by that particular maker? Is it plentiful or somewhat rare? Anything you can tell me about this watch will be welcome.

Your letter describes a type of repeater watch made during the 1800-1900 period.

We have no reference for the number 152821. 0.750 is the designation for 18 karat.

Le Coultre supplied many movements of the style appearing in Figure 4B to which your letter refers.

These movements, or parts, were bought by manufacturers who finished and cased them and either put their names or the name of the store to whom they sold it on the movement, cuvette, or dial.

How many were m a d e ? These watches were made in Switzerland during the period when Americans became conscious of railroad quality watches. It was when American watch manufacturers were enjoying their greatest success. It was during a time that the Swiss lost their important American market and found that the best way to compete was to make novelty type watches.

Many quarter repeater, calendar, and o t h e r non-time-telling only watches were made during that period.

(Abe Secofsky)

623

AN APRON

From: James J. Jimmy, 2672 Jelly-bean Lane, Jamestown, NY 12345

In a shoe box full of clock parts formerly owned by my grandfather, who was a watchmaker, I found this quite decorative pierced and engraved piece of brass. I am assuming that it is from a clock. Can you tell me what it is and how old it is?

The piece in your photograph is indeed a clock part. It is known as an "apron," and is described by DeCarle in his *Watch & Clock Encyclopedia* as "the decorative piece attached to the pallet cock of some of the old bracket clocks."

Unlike the decorative watch cock, which performs the function of holding the upper verge pivot, the apron served no useful purpose except to cover up an area that is not particularly attractive.

It would be my guess that your apron is from a late 18th Century Dutch clock. (Charles Terwilliger)

* * *

ELGIN WATCH

From: Wm. Mackie, 2216 W. Club View Dr., Glendale, WI 53209

I have in my possession an Elgin pocket watch. It is a 14K case and has micrometer time adjustment and seems to be of superior quality workmanship.

It is marked Elgin Nat'l Watch Co. Serial #1158855.

From this serial number, could you be able to give me any history of this watch?

Your Elgin watch movement is a fine example of early railroad quality and was manufactured about 1882-1884. The gold watch case is a desired and sought after "box" type.

According to the serial number of the movement, the following information is available: The movement is a convertible type, which means it could be used in hunting cases as well as in open face cases. Convertible movements are very collectible and desirable. Your movement is 16s, leverset, 15j, nickel finish and is a Model #2.

The first recorded serial number is 701,000 produced about 1880, and the last serial number was 6,337,000 produced about 1895.

This certainly is a nice fine quality example of an Elgin and you should be proud to own it. (Arthur I. Silver)

* * *

UNUSUAL SHIP'S CLOCK

From: Jonathan Allison, 438 Washington Trust Building, Washington, PA 15301

Enclosed is a photograph of an unusual ship's clock that I own and I am wondering if you can give me some information on it.

This is a brass (it may have been chrome originally) non-striking 8-day Seth Thomas ship's clock, 3¼" deep with a 6" dial. The movement is run by two main springs each wound separately.

Frictioned on the second hand shaft inside is a black bakelite gear in the shape of a comma (,).

As the gear rotates it lifts a knife switch out of the slot of an electric switch attached to the plate. When it slides off the tail of the comma the knife falls into the slot and makes electric contact. As the comma gear continues to turn it lifts the knife out of the slot and contact is broken. Contact is made every 60 seconds.

There are wires running from the knife switch, one to the inside of each plug on the top of the clock. A wire can then be attached to the outside of each of the plugs on the top of the clock.

I have been unable to learn what type of ship's clock this is; what it is called; or the purpose it served on the ship, or what era it was in use.

Your ship's clock is a Seth Thomas 10A, 8-day model, ca. 1918. The movement was designed with two large barrels to drive the cylindrical drum in various types of recording instruments, such as, tide gauges, anemometers (wind speed), barographs, Navy Zig-Zag Control Timers, etc. Some were fitted with hands and dials and were used as Deck and Engine Room clocks. The mechanism was equipped with an external gear, generally on the center wheel arbor which meshed with a gear on the cylinder shaft to drive the recording drum in a clockwise direction.

Because of its adaptability, some (as yours) were fitted with an electrical make or break circuit device. In order to successfully carry out surveying and mapping operations, solar observations, and scientific experiments in remote areas, an audible time signal was necessary. To meet those needs, a break circuit device and electrical contact system was installed in some movements.

The closing of the circuit energizes the coil of a sounder, bell or relay, producing a distinct sound or tick. Thus, by connecting up a set of head phones or the sounder, a remote observer could receive an audible time signal.

Some were made to make contact every 60 seconds while in others the 59th tooth was omitted, so when the circuit was operating, the sound or tick was produced for each second, but when it reached the 59th, the break was for a longer duration so the operator knew when the minute began. In others, the 29th second was also omitted or any combination up to 60 may be had, depending on the particular requirement. (Marvin E. Whitney)

* * *

SELF-WINDING CLOCK

From: Jim Stephan, 5184 Hidden Hills Tr., Stone Mountain, GA 30088

I have just received my late uncle's clock. He worked for Western Union and they gave it to him when he retired. I am really interested in learning more about this clock. It was made by the Self-Winding Clock Co., NY. The card inside states it is a 120-beat brass bob pendulum. From assorted numbers I guess it was manufactured circa 1936. The movement number is 161859. The clock weighs approximately 24 lbs. and the case is 21" x 21" x 5". There are cards indicating how to hook it up to Western Union lines but presently it is running on batteries and winds itself every hour.

Can anyone recommend books to read in the NAWCC Library that de-

Mr. Allison's Seth Thomas ship's clock.

The self-winding clock owned by Jim Stephan.

scribe this clock? I am also interested in just the general number of these clocks manufactured, t h e i r history, how many exist today, etc.

Your clock is typical of those manufactured by the Self-Winding Clock Company for use in Leased Service Time Systems, as supplied to Western Union and others. These were synchronized by means of daily signals sent via telegraph lines which assisted in maintaining a reasonable degree of accuracy in timekeeping.

The system was invented by Chester H. Pond of Brooklyn, NY, in 1881, and the earliest model was manufactured for S-WCC by Seth Thomas, with the front plate inscribed "Patented Nov. 17, 83." While the first model employed a 3-pole rotary motor, the later units which were made by S-WCC employed a ratchet type motor for simplicity and greater reliability. It has been estimated that over 150,000 units were in use by the year 1900, so it would appear that an estimate of the total number of clocks made would be virtually impossible!

The Self-Winding Clock Company was in business from the 1880's to shortly after World War II, manufacturing wall, mantel, tower, streetpost, and gallery styles, and even included a few models of an Astronomical Regulator employing a Gerry Gravity Escapement. The movements were well constructed, spring p o w e r e d , with hourly rewinding which provided relatively uniform spring tension. Two #6 dry cells powered the rewinding motor, with a useful life of approximately a year. Five different movement types were made during the evolution of the product line, including in the primary series, Programming and Synchronizing options, and in the secondary or Master/Slave systems, a series of Watchmen's Time Detectors. Many of the master systems are still in use today, chiefly for the program devices which would be costly to replace.

Additional information is available from the following sources: Catalog reprint and set-up instructions: Self Winding Publications, PO Box 7704, Long Beach, CA 90807; and Technical and Mechanical Information (approximately 6 pages) : The Modern Clock, by Ward L. Goodrich. (M. Swetsky)

* * *

THE LETTER G

From: Gregory E. Hannah, RR #1, Hannon, Ont., Canada L0R 1P0

I have a 400-day, standard looking clock with a glass dome. The back plate is mentioned in "Horolovar 400 Day Clock Repair Guide," by Charles Terwilliger, 8th edition. It is described on p. 73 by a "G" as the manufacturer. A "G" is stamped on the bottom left hand corner with a serial #78514. Do you know the manufacturer's name, clock vintage, or any history?

About your interest in the meaning of the letter G that appears in the lower left hand corner of Plate 1146 of the *Horolovar Repair Guide*. I wish I knew!

You will also find similar letters H, J, F, and S (I think that's all) for the same Jahresuhrenfabrik clock that was made about 1908. They are all illustrated in the 9th Edition of the Guide.

The only thing I can figure out is that the letters were "keys" to importers' orders, in case there were any come-backs. Since the movements were otherwise exactly alike throughout, the letter would identify it as having been shipped to a specific company. Just a guess — until someone comes up with a better idea! (Charles Terwilliger)

JNᴼ JOHNSON, LIVERPOOL

From: Fred C. Grotenrath, 2201 W. Green Tree Rd., Milwaukee, WI 53209

I hope you will help me on the following questions: (1) What information is available on a Jnᵒ Johnson, watchmaker, Liverpool? (2) Of what design were the original hands? (3) Does this type of watch justify having hinge work, movement cleaned, etc.?

The dial is approximately 46.4 mm diameter, porcelain with fine Roman numerals on the chapter and arabic numerals on the second bit chapter. The hands are Louis XIV in brass or gold finish, second bit is slender straight blued.

The case is sterling silver with hallmark "S" that is similar to 1813-1814, includes lion passant and a lion head. The initials stamped J J and serialized #30087. The glass is double lunette — cut top (Britten dkictionary). The movement is lever escapement, one bridge, balance screws. It appears the balance wheel is jewelled. The power is a chain fusee.

The keywind is inserted in the back at about the 10 O'clock position (from the back). The hands set with same key from dial front.

The movement is serialized #30087 same as case. The name Jnᵒ Johnson is machine engraved on movement plate with Liverpool included. The movement is all brass; the single escape wheel bridge is engraved. The balance wheel has balance screws and adjustment lever. The word "detach" marked on the bridge, and the word "lever" appears on the movement.

The case has three hinges. (1) Bezel hinge at 9 position. (2) Movement hinges out from 12 position with a clip arrangement at 6 position. (3) Dust cover has no hinging. (4) Back cover hinged at 12 position.

The movement is further protected by a drawn brass cover that has two studs projecting from the back plate. The cover has a spring steel slide catch similar to a drawn bow (bow and arrow) to lock back cover to movement. The watch is running. I wonder if having it cleaned, the hinge repaired, and finding out what hands were used would make it suitable for a gift to my grandson.

According to Liverpool town clerk, Mr. T. Alker, his records indicate that there was a watchmaker named Joseph Johnson working in Liverpool in 1814 whose shop was located at 1 Blake Street.

Regarding the design of the original hands. Many watchmakers of that period used Double Swell spade hands. You may find American style spade hands are good replacements as they are available with the square hole.

Because the watch is in running condition the cost of cleaning should be modest, and recommended if you are considering giving the watch as a gift.

There are several members advertising in the MART that they do watch repairs. Others who are casemakers can repair the broken hinge, which is a relatively minor type of repair. (Abe Secofsky)

* * *

AN OLDER OG

From: Edward E. Coing, Sedgewood Club, R.D. 12, Carmel, NY 10512

The Chauncey Jerome OG clock described on pp. 508-509 of the NAWCC BULLETIN, October 1981, fascinate me and makes me wonder if I may have an older clock since mine seems to have been made in Bristol, CT.

My clock has a 24-hour brass movement driven by a weight, with another weight for the hourly strike.

The name of the printer appears at the bottom of the label below the ornate border of the instructions, as follows: Elihu Geer, Job and Card Printer, 26½ State Street, Hartford, Conn.

I shall appreciate any information you may be able to give me as to date of manufacture, and if Jeromes & Co. is the same as Jerome Manufacturing Co., or Chauncey Jerome.

Your clock is older than those of "Jerome Manufacturing Co.," which started operations in 1845, and "Chauncey Jerome," which name was used from 1841 through 1845. Kenneth Roberts, in his well researched and documented *The Contributions of Joseph Ives to Connecticut Clock Technology*, at p. 161 states: "The firm of

Jeromes & Co. is believed to have been the same as C. & N. Jerome." Brooks Palmer, in *A Treasury of American Clocks* at p. 348, indicates Jeromes & Co. operated in Bristol 1841-1844. The firm of C. & N. Jerome was in operation under that name up to 1840.

Apparently, Jeromes & Co. used two designs of 30-hour, weight-driven, brass movements. Your clock has the older of these two — the three-bar, parallel bar movement, both plates of which have three vertical support bars, or members, and two horizontal bars at top and bottom only. The later movement used by this firm had two full-length vertical bars, on the extreme left and right of the plates, with the relatively common "T-Frame" structure in the center of the plates.

The earliest Jerome 30-hour brass OG's known at present are the models with the business card label of C. & N. Jerome which probably predates 1839. These clocks had unpainted zinc, circular dials with black lettering. Your brass embossed OG dial probably was introduced about 1839, and was used on later Jeromes & Co. OG's with the "T-Frame" movement described above. One can only opine as to the exact year of manufacture of your clock, but I will state 1839-1840.

The fact that the label of your clock was printed by Elihu Geer while at the 26½ State St., Hartford address is additional support for the above view. At p. 199 of *The Book of American Clocks*, Palmer lists Geer's earliest address as 26 State St. for the years 1838-1847, and does not even list the 26½ State St. address.

(Amerst Ed. Huson)

* * *

AMERICAN WATCH CO.

From: C. D. James, Flat 28, Springhill Ct., Sutton Rd., Walsall WS1 2PB, W. Mids, England

Could you please supply me with any information on an A m e r i c a n pocket watch which I have failed to find in either Townsend or Shugart & Engle?

Details: O/F, 16S, sterling silver cased, A.W.Co., 2814. On the dial,

American Watch Co. The numerals are Arabic. The movement is ¾ plate, SW, LS. Serial #1,260,007, which I assume from Waltham production dates and numbers puts it at 1878.

I am puzzled by the facts that on the back plate is stamped or engraved: Excelsior No. 2 / Made at Waltham Mass for / Howard & Co. Fifth Ave. N.Y. / and the escapement, Woerd's Patents.

I have failed to find Excelsior No. 2 model for the American Watch Co. and also what Woerd's Patents are. Is it possible that Howard & Co., Fifth Ave., NY, was a store or large jeweler for whom this particular type of watch was made?

I would be grateful for any help or information that you can send me.

Your watch was made by the American Watch Company. Probably it was made to a special order for the Howard C o m p a n y, of New York City. American watch factories, in general, would engrave almost anything that a customer would request on a watch, if a certain minimum number of watches was ordered at a time. The "Excelsior No. 2," and "Made at Waltham, Mass. for Howard & Co. Fifth Ave. N. Y." would come under this category. I have run across the name Howard & Co., of New York City, before, but do not know if it was a retail or a wholesale establishment. I do not believe that it was connected in any way with E. Howard & Co., the manufacturer of the Howard watches.

I am puzzled by the serial number of your watch. According to the Waltham serial number list, watch #1,260,-007 should have been an 18-size, full-plate watch of the 1877 model. There are a few errors in the serial number list, and perhaps this is one of them.

Mr. C. V. Woerd was a long-time employee of the American Watch Company, and was superintendent of that company from 1876 to 1883. Mr. Woerd held many patents on both watchmaking machinery, and on improvements and a c c e s s o r i e s for watches. Among these were patents on watch regulators, and on stem-winding watches in general. It is not possible to tell which of these patents applied to your watch. (A. E. Mathews)

Mr. Plumlee's watch.

BAR MOVEMENT WATCH

From: Hugh W. Plumlee, 4100 Weeks Park Lane, 129, Wichita Falls, TX 76308

Enclosed is a picture of a watch movement along with some very poor sketches and some details about the case and movement. It is a Bar movement, similar to one pictured in a book by T. P. Camerer Cuss, page 63, Plate 71, "Geneva Movement," Circa 1840.

As you can see, the balance wheel has a solid rim and Compensation Curb is used for temperature regulation. The shock resistant is the Parachute type.

The movement is a little larger than 18 size, has 13 jewels counting the roller jewel, and would equal modern 15-jewel movements, except the pallets of the fork are metal. The movement is some kind of white (heavy) metal that has been "brass" plated. However, the top sides of the bars are polished silver color, as well as the dial side of the full plate.

I have been unable to locate anything to help identify the maker and age in any of the library books here.

Your watch is of the 1840-1850 period. This date agrees with your reference.

There is a record of a Charles Montandon who worked in Switzerland during that period. There is also a record of the firm of Charles Montandon & Girard, of that period.

The firm exported watches to the U.S. of similar description to yours. Many with engraved covers with harbor and country scenes in engine-turned cases.

Bar type movements, made popular during the early 19th Century, were a favorite type of construction for two reasons. For the well dressed man, the thinner case bulged less when worn in the vest pocket. Also, the watch weighed less.

Regarding the hallmarking in the case: Your sketch is similar to the marks that would normally appear in an English hallmarked case. The date letter you mention (R) and the old English style is the 1852 London hallmark. This date corresponds generally to the approximate date of manufacture of the watch.

Since we can not explain the presence of English hallmarks in the case, it is possible that the movements were cased in London and the Swiss manufacturer's name was engraved on the case, since the movement could never pass as anything but Swiss.

(Abe Secofsky)

BOOK REVIEW

SILVERSMITHS AND CLOCKMAKERS OF FULTON COUNTY, PENNSYLVANIA 1785-1900
John H. Nelson

30 pages, 8½" x 5½", paper covers, 16 photographs and facsimilies of advertisements. Available from the Fulton County Historical Society, Box 115, McConnellsburg, PA 17233. Price $3.54, postpaid.

This little book covers information found on 28 silversmiths, watchmakers, clockmakers, and jewelers who worked in Fulton County, in south-central Pennsylvania. Included are three clockmakers, although no clocks are known for two of the three makers. Repairers are distinguished by the terms "clocksmith" and "watchsmith." The facsimilies of advertisements are interesting. Information on the Sherry & Byram tower clock formerly in the county court house is also included. (Donald J. Summar)

* * *

FRENCH CLOCKS THE WORLD OVER
Part III — From the Louis Philippe style to the Modern clock and the French Provinces
and
CLOCKS THE WORLD OVER
Netherlands, Belgium, England, Scotland, United States, Canada
Tardy

526 pages, 9½" x 12½", over 1300 illustrations — 74 in color, hard covers. Available in the USA from horological booksellers. Price $95.00.

This is the third in a new, four-volume publication, a very much expanded and better organized extension of *La Pendule Francaise*, first published about 35 years ago. The text, originally in French, is now in both French and English. (Part I was reviewed in June 1982 BULLETIN; Part II in June 1983 BULLETIN.) Part IV, soon to be off the press, will cover clocks in Switzerland, Germany, Northern and Eastern Europe, the Mediterranean countries, and Asia.

The present volume includes Chapter XIV — The Louis-Philippe and Napoleon III style (1830-1870); Chapter XV — Late 19th Century Clocks; Chapter XVI — The "Modern Style" (1890-1920) (there is no Chapter XVII, which is undoubtedly a copy editor's mistake, but the missing years, 1921-1924, were unimportant; XVIII — 1925 and after; XIX — The French Provinces; XX — Netherlands; XXI — Belgium; XXII — England; XXIII — Scotland; XXIV — Ireland; XXV — United States; and XXVI — Canada. Each chapter begins with a brief history of the country's clockmaking.

As noted in previous reviews, the original *La Pendule Francaise* was the first book ever published that made it possible to date many otherwise unidentified French clocks by the design of the case ornaments, the construction of the movement, the type of escapement, or the style of the dial and hands. However, the book had little use as a reference, because the pages were not numbered. The new series has numbered pages, is considerably expanded, and has brought order out of chaos.

Chapters XIV-XVIII, as noted, cover French clocks, 1830 to 1925 and after. These later periods of French horology have been considerably expanded and contain a larger variety of clocks. The development of mass production and the manufacturing of cheaper clocks for a wider market, at the same time that clocks of high precision, made of rare materials, continued to be made, is noted.

At the end of Chapter XIV, as after previous chapters, there is a section on hands, dials, case making, marbles, bronzes, and movements and escapements, the latter illustrated by 42 drawings and 5 photographs of movements, calendar wheel trains and escapements by Brocot, Roret, Moinet,

LePaute, Pierret, Japy, James, Wagner, Robert, and others from clocks in Paris and London exhibitions of 1839, 1862, and 1867. (The text under the rack and snail, and the text under the count wheel striking movements are unfortunately reversed.)

The French Provinces, Chapter XIX, are very well illustrated with many different styles of clock movements, cases, and pendulums. There are 76 tall case clocks illustrated, and although it is difficult to tell the difference between a clock from Burgundy and one from Champagne, some generalities are possible such as that a typical Morbier case, in addition to a bulbous center, has a flat top. It's interesting that movements in clocks from the Vosges area, so near to Germany, are very much like the movements made in Germany.

Clocks of The Netherlands, Chapter XX, are very thoroughly covered in its 80 pages, including 4 in color, showing one of the largest variety of Dutch clocks illustrated in any book. Included are domestic iron clocks, lantern clocks, "The Hague" table and bracket clocks, long case clocks, including "Amsterdam" type, notary clocks, Groningen and Frisian Stoelkloks and Staartkloks, as well as Stoeltjeskloks, Stoofkloks, Schippertje, and Zaan, Dikkop, Twente and Ruempol types.

Belgium clocks, Chapter XXI, has 48 pages, 9 in color. Iron wall, mantel, table, and bracket clocks are illustrated, as are 73 tall case clocks. Only one tall case movement is shown.

Chapter XXII on English clocks occupies 98 pages, 7 in color, the latter picturing two ornate musical automaton clocks recently sold by Sotheby. A wide variety of types appear including lantern, table, bracket, mantel, Eureka, Act of Parliament, elephant, strut, musical, 9 skeletons, 64 tall case, and an astronomical movement by Shortt. There are 17 carriage clocks by Vulliamy, Cole, McCabe, Dent, Frodsham, Kulberg, Payne, and others. One page is devoted to designs of English clock hands.

Chapter XXIII, Clocks of Scotland, is devoted chiefly to tall case clocks. In 10 pages, 10 clocks are illustrated, 7 showing details of dial and/or movements.

Chapter XXIV covers clocks of Ireland with illustrations of tall case and bracket clocks, and one carriage clock by McMaster & Son.

Chapter XXV devotes 36 pages to Clocks of the United States with illustrations chiefly from The Smithsonian Institution, but also from the Metropolitan Museum of Art and others. This chapter will be of more interest to those who don't have other books available to them which describe American horology in more detail.

Finally, Chapter XXVI is devoted to Canadian clocks, the 14 illustrated credited to the Treherne Museum in Manitoba. One of them is a gravity clock, known to have had its origin in England.

The three volumes of *French Clocks the World Over* published so far are an indispensable source of information that should be in every museum, on the shelves of every knowledgeable antique dealer, and in the hands of everyone interested in clocks, not just French clocks. However, the major flaw in this extensive work is still the lack of an index. Photographs are captioned, but not numbered, so references can be made only by page number or by page number and position on the page, which is unnecessarily awkward. (Charles Terwilliger)

*

Because of my personal interest in novelty clocks or clocks that have other major features beside telling time, Part III of *La Pendule Francaise* has been the most interesting part of this Tardy series for me to review. Those with similar interest will find a large number of novelty clocks in just this one volume:

Cathedral clocks, some with supplementary water fountain, windmill and semaphore movements, pages 16-21, 122; Inkstand, 26; Moving ships and birds under domes, including drawing of the mechanism, 32, 33, 61; Picture clocks with views of musical movements, 34, 35, 124; Industrial clocks, 93, 108, 109, 144; Jacob Petit school, 49-51, 127, 128; Watch holders, 52, 148; Horizontal pendulum, 136, 137; Rotary pendulum, 54, 82, 94, 129; Mantel regulators, 62, 63, 135; Skeleton, 56, 134; Cartier, 150; To-and-fro pendulum, 86; Battery, 57, 101; Night,

58, 59; Mystery, 59, 83 (with photograph of movement), 107, 110, 115, 116, 119, 138, 468; Automaton, 60, 61; Inclined plane, 110; Carriage, 66, 90; 104, 145, 452-457, 479; Balloon, 67; Falling ball, 110; Swinging pendulum, 82; Perpetual motion, 91, 92, 111, 146; Lalique, 118, 119; Atmos, 115, 139; Crystal, 149; Revolving Map, 151; Climbing, 157; Double-faced hanging pendulums, 181. (C.T.)

* * *

E. HOWARD & CO. WATCHES
1858-1903
GEORGE E. TOWNSEND

48 pages, 11" x 8¼", soft covers, many illustrations. Published 1984 by Heart of America Press, Box 9808, Kansas City, MO 64134. Price $8.00.

Those who collect American watches, and Howard watches in particular, need no introduction to the writings of the late George E. Townsend, as he was considered this country's leading authority on earlier American pocket watches. This book is a posthumous effort which contains all that Townsend had assiduously collected and should be considered the most authoritative source on the products of this very early American maker of high quality watches.

This book contains a history of the company, description of the movements, size designations, serial productions and dates of manufacture. Also, there is a casing and comment that all movements left the factory uncased, and the various casemakers who made cases expressly for these odd-sized movements are listed.

Especial movements by Howard, such as the use of the resilient escapement, are noted and explained. Townsend has made many very fine drawings of parts of the movements which should help the collector and repairer, giving dimensions of various critical parts, and he has included drawings and dimensions of all staffs. Reproductions from Howard material catalogs are included as well with detailed comments by the author. There are charts of specifications for the various movements and the details of the various series running by serial numbers, pages of hand-drawn fine illustrations

of parts not seen in Howard material catalogs. Also, all known Howard movements are pictured. The details of hands, hole-size, color, and shape, are listed in detail.

To this the publisher, Roy Ehrhardt, in his own right a leading authority on American watches and price guides, has added a list of current values. For the collector of American watches, and to Howard collectors especially, this book is a MUST, a comprehensive effort, and should be in every American watch collector's library.

(Henry B. Fried)

* * *

CLOCK MAKING FOR THE WOODWORKER
WAYNE LOUIS KADAR

184 pages, 7" x 9", 295 illustrations. Published by TAB Books, Inc., Blue Ridge Summit, PA 17214. Price $11.50.

For the clock hobbyist who dreams of rehousing a favorite, caseless movement, but feels that he has only modest skills and knowledge, this book should point the way toward realizing some of his goals.

The author is an industrial teacher in a secondary school whose specialty is cabinet making and basic woodworking. His methods are clear and simple.

The projects' requirements range from jig-saws, portable power saws, measuring devices, table saws, rasps, files, drills, clamps and bench, and powered devices.

The chapters include Clock Movements, The Dial or Clock Face, Kitchen Clocks, Mantel Clocks, Wall Clocks, Quickie Clocks [novelty clocks], Selling Your Work, Suppliers, Glossary and Index.

The instructions include the construction of a floor clock case for a chiming clock movement, electrics, construction of boxed clocks, decorative, form and shaped clock cases, pan, fruit-form clocks, sport motif cases, and other novel items. Converting photographs and picture scenes into clocks is also covered.

The instructions are good and easy to follow. For the watch or clockmaker, this book offers simple, basic instructions and methods which nevertheless are acceptable to the experienced woodworker. (Henry B. Fried)

CHAPTER HIGHLIGHTS

Total membership on September 1, 1984 — 32,576

First accession number on September 1, 1984 — 85,611

NOTE!
BULLETIN DEADLINE

February issue — December 1
April issue — February 1
June issue — April 1
August issue — June 1
October issue — August 1
December issue — October 1

Above is our deadline schedule for accepting Chapter reports for publication. We will publish Chapter reports for meetings held during the three months prior to the deadline. For example, reports for January, February, and March meetings, if received by April 1, will be published in the June BULLETIN.

1. PHILADELPHIA

Meeting Calendar
December 2, 1984
January 6, 1985
February 24, 1985

We met at the Holiday Inn, King of Prussia, PA, on May 20th. This being our election meeting, the following Officers were installed: President, Cy Felheimer; Vice-President, Lee Davis; Secretary, Cecelia Sweisford; and T r e a s u r e r , Peg Hornberger. Our speaker was Jack Shaull; his subject was Andrew Marlow, an accomplished cabinet maker, who resided in York, PA. In addition to full-sized furniture he made miniatures — chairs, other furniture, and clocks. He started this miniature cabinetry at the age of 23 and made countless miniature chairs for Christmas presents. His small clock reproductions were done from photographs, and his proportions and appearances are beautiful. His movements were procured from New Haven at 25 or 30¢ apiece. There were 15 different clocks made and 16 variations of banjo clocks. Some books written by Mr. Marlow are: *Fine Furniture For the Amateur Cabinetmaker; Clas-*

Chapter #1's May meeting speaker Jack Shaull. (Sweisford photo)

sic *Furniture Projects, Good Furniture You Can Make Yourself,* and *Cabinetmaker's Treasury.* Following World War II, Mr. Marlow discontinued making miniature clocks, but remained active with furniture. He passed away in February, 1984.

Jack showed slides of Mr. Marlow's work, along with some actual pieces, and presented a very informative and interesting talk.

Fred Breitinger's workshop in clock repair problems continues to be very well attended with the innovation of different members presenting solutions to, or ways of conquering, clock troubles.

---

4. SOUTHERN CALIFORNIA

Meeting Calendar
Third Saturday — Each Month

Following an hour of display and ladies' tables, our May 19th meeting was called to order by Chapter Pres-

ident Leo Severns, in Paramount Park, CA, with 135 attendants.

Program Chairman Bill Givens presented an excellent NAWCC slide/tape program, "Animated & Complicated Watches of the Sandoz Collection," by Henry Cole.

*

At our June 16th meeting, with an attendance of 103, Bill Givens presented his original program, "Developing The Perfect Timekeeper." After a period of discussion on points to consider in building a perfect timepiece, he divided the assembly, and asked that each group plan and report their clock of perfection.

New Officers elected for the coming year are: Dr. Ben Honning, President; Greg Joseph, Vice-President; Dorothy Severns, Secretary; and George Laughlin, Treasurer. Tave Krohn, Bob Smith, and Norman Gould were elected 2-year Directors to serve with 2nd-year Director Bob Davidson.

---

5. SAN FRANCISCO — DR. W. BARCLAY STEPHENS MEMORIAL

Meeting Calendar
Second Sunday — MART Months
Except First Sunday in May

The July 8th meeting, held at the Student Union Building of the College of San Mateo, CA, featured a fascinating slide program on Breguet watches presented by Joe Spranza. All of the slides were of Breguet watches that once belonged to the late Ralph Shermund.

The slides depicted several of Breguet's "subscription" series watches; a pocket watch smaller than a U.S. penny; a lovely ring watch; and many other beautiful one-of-a-kind examples of Breguet's workmanship, all in superb condition.

One slide showed a unique enamel table clock with music box and a matching watch. The clock does not function unless the watch is placed in its proper position as the front "dial" of the clock. This rare piece is pictured on page 228 of the book *The Art of Breguet,* by George Daniels.

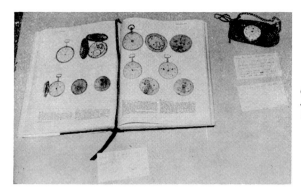

One Breguet watch
displayed at Chapter #5's
July meeting.
(Armack photo)

Joe gave a brief biography of Abram Louis Breguet (1747-1823), a native of Switzerland, who spent most of his working life in Paris, with the exception of a few years during the French Revolution when he lived in England and Switzerland. Breguet was an extremely inventive man; some of his more unusual inventions are the automatic winding watch, a perpetual calendar, ruby cylinders for watch escapements, and a "pendule sympathetique" in which a specially-built watch is wound and r e g u l a t e d by its "mother" clock.

Seth Finkelstein (l e f t) and Joe Spranza, Chapter #5's July speaker, appear deeply involved in a discussion of Breguet watches. (Armack photo)

6. GREAT LAKES

Meeting Calendar
December 8, 1984

The July 14th meeting was held at the Mayflower Meeting House in Plymouth, MI. The program, from National, was an outstanding presentation by J. Carter Harris, Curator of the NAWCC Museum, on Pennsylvania Shelf Clocks 1790-1850. The slide lecture illuminated some of the elements of Pennsylvania clocks that are peculiar to clocks made in that region.

12. WASHINGTON, DC

Our meeting of May 20th was held at the Holiday Inn, Dulles International Airport, Stirling, VA. Our speaker was Norman Langmaid. His presentation was a captivating travelog which held everyone's attention. With Norman, there are no dull moments. In pursuit of his primary interest — CLOCKS — Norman has traveled to many parts of the globe. Many times he could be found in England, searching its cities and countryside seeking clocks: old clocks, broken clocks, good and bad clocks, whole clocks or not. He has discovered a number of real prizes in his never-ending pursuit of the works of the horological masters. Being gifted in this regard he has restored a good number of his newly found treasures. One would surely label him successful. The NAWCC has bestowed upon him the honor of "FELLOW."

Dr. Leonard Weiss (left) discusses early watches with Chapter #13's President Chuck Roeser at the May meeting.

13. WESTERN NEW YORK

Meeting Calendar
January 20, 1985

Our Chapter met at the Sacred Heart Social Center, Batavia, NY, on May 20th. A short discussion revealed that 23 of our Chapter members were planning to attend the National Convention in Indianapolis, IN.

Dr. Leonard Weiss, European clock and watch enthusiast, gave a most interesting talk and slide program, "18th Century Watchmaking." He has devoted much of his time to researching the development of early watches. A book he has written, *Watchmaking in England 1760-1820*, has just been published, and to the watch collector it may be a valuable aid. After the talk there was a discussion on early watches.

15. SOUTHWESTERN

Meeting Calendar
Third Saturday — Each Month

The May 19th meeting was held at the LBJ Federal Park across the Perdenales River from the LBJ ranch house, near Fredericksburg, TX. President Overton emphasized members volunteering their time and talents to make all our Chapter meetings successful. We toured the LBJ Federal Park and Ranch by bus, and, much to our delight, saw some antique clocks in some of the houses.

17. CAROLINA

Meeting Calendar
First Sunday — BULLETIN Months

We met on June 3rd at the Holiday Inn, Winston-Salem, NC. Jarvis Warren offered the invocation and members remembered departed Charlie Robinson with a moment of silence. A buffet luncheon was served.

It was noted that Max Dwiggins had recruited 5 new members to our Chapter. Alice McCall announced two more contributions to the National Endowment Fund. Suggested Constitution and Bylaw changes were then reviewed and it was determined to send out ballots. The program was by Ray Troutman who gave a slide presentation on "Old World Clocks."

20. MINNESOTA — OSCAR T. LANG MEMORIAL

Meeting Calendar
November 18, 1984

On July 21st we held a dinner meeting at JAX Cafe in Minneapolis, MN. Dick Porter, Don Empson, and Irv Schneider demonstrated some aspects of clock and watch repair. Kenneth and Darlene Vergin from Chapter #127 had a display of very fine watches.

During the business meeting, Don Empson discussed efforts to develop a history of horological activity in Minnesota. As our main program, Don Hoke from the Milwaukee Public Museum presented, "Watchmaking at Waltham," a pictorial discussion of the manufacturing of watches at Waltham. We all enjoyed this presentation.

Tony Gohl (left)
discusses watchmaking
with Chapter #20's speaker,
Don Hoke.

25. NEW JERSEY

Meeting Calendar
November 10, 1984
February 9, 1985
April 20, 1985

Fine weather greeted Chapter #25 members and their guests at the picnic meeting held at Harbor Hills Picnic Grove, Mount Freedom, NJ, on June 16th. The 235 people in attendance represented a good turnout.

Several interesting clocks were displayed. One of these was certainly the steeple-on-steeple wagon spring clock (see photo). Also of note was an Ansonia chime clock in a banjo case. It had a round lower section with an etched glass tablet. The case was unusually deep and heavy, to accommodate the chime movement.

—————————>

This 8-day steeple on steeple wagon spring power clock is a shining example of a timepiece made between 1844 and 1848 by the successful partnership of John Birge and Thomas Fuller. The clock was a focal point among displays at Chapter #25's meeting. (BIZ photo)

30. CHEROKEE

Meeting Calendar
December 16, 1984

Our Chapter meeting was held in the Cherokee Room of the Marriott Hotel on June 23rd, with 64 in attendance.

After the business meeting we had a very interesting slide/tape program from National, "8-Day Wooden Works Shelf Clocks," by W. L. Wadleigh, Jr.

We will be hosting the 10th M-K-O Regional in November and there was discussion on that.

Bob Higgins, 1984 President, holding the Chapter #31 Charter which 1959 President Earl Hackett obtained for the first Pacific-Northwest Chapter.

31. PACIFIC-NORTHWEST

Meeting Calendar
Third Saturday — Each Month
Except February, April,
October, December

Our May 25th meeting, held at Country Bills Restaurant, was our Silver Anniversary meeting, having been chartered in May 1959. To honor the occasion, founder Earl Hackett, and Charter members Albert Odmark and Lyle Flaherty attended, along with Mrs. Gertrude Odmark.

Earl recalled the early days of the NAWCC, the need for a Chapter in the Pacific-Northwest, discussions with Jim Gibbs of National, the 1955 tour to England, how difficult it was in 1956 and 1957 to contact people in the Northwest, and how finally enough NAWCC members were contacted to obtain the Charter, presented by Earl T. Strickler in Columbia. In addition to Albert Odmark and Lyle Flaherty, some other first members were: Harley Prior, at whose home the first meeting was held, Lester Parker, Charley Schubert, Bob Milspaugh, Bryson Moore, and Jim Chisum. Earl then detailed his work in starting Chapter #50 in the Seattle area. The Puget Sound Charter was presented at the National in South Carolina; and the formation of the Inland Empire Chapter, whose Charter was presented at the National in Cleveland.

Earl then described his own horological interests, which leaned mainly toward watches. At one time he owned over 10,000 watches. He mentioned that it appeared to him that clocks were the main thrust of the members of the Chapters he started, as well as the National itself. He closed his remarks with the fact that he also taught watch and clock repair classes to NAWCC members. He was, and remains, a remarkably dedicated member of the NAWCC, and our Chapter.

We were treated to the Chris Bailey slide/tape program from National, "American Clockmaking, F r o m A Craft To An Industry," on 19th Century clockmaking in the Bristol-Waterbury-New Haven areas, and the work of Elias Ingraham, his family business, and the eventual formation of the American Clock and Watch Museum in Bristol, as well as a "who's who" of the clockmakers and merchants of the Connecticut factories. This is an excellent program with superb examples of the period, and we recommend it be shown as soon as possible at Chapter meetings.

*

Our regular meeting date was changed to June 9th in order to have Dr. Winthrop Dolan, a Mathematics Professor at Linfield College in McMinneville, OR, as a speaker. He spoke about his hobby, Sundials. Sundials were first used as timekeepers about 1500 BC, and the original "shadow caster" type sundial remained virtually unchanged for 2900 years.

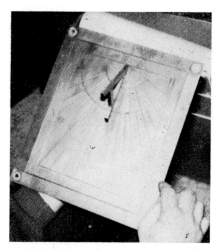

The "Shadow Caster" type sundial as explained by Dr. Dolan at Chapter #31's June meeting.

As the old saying "fingers before forks" goes, so it was with sundials before clocks and watches, according to Dr. Dolan. He demonstrated a shadow caster with a sundial made from one sheet of 8½ x 11 notebook paper, and explained that size can provide greater accuracy. On one huge sundial in India, the shadow will move one foot in five minutes, which would allow very distinct segments for the minutes.

Dr. Dolan then showed a model of the "polar" or equatorial type sundial. This model was made from pieces of a plastic bottle, and thread. The "polar" type dial, when properly set up, can be extremely accurate. If the shadow caster of the "polar" type, in this case a string, is parallel to the Earth's axis, and aimed toward the North Star, it can be much more accurate than the conventional type, and less subject to the variant effect of the earth's tilt. This type of sundial was invented around 1400 AD, and represented the first change in technology since the original. For another 200 to 250 years, this type was the most accurate timekeeper, and until the invention of the pendulum in the 17th Century its accuracy surpassed the verge and foliot escapement clocks and watches.

Dr. Dolan then described various systems to account for the "seasonal"

hour, or the effects of the earth's tilt. At the equator, the hour remains constant at 60 minutes. In Alaska, for example, the seasonal hour might range from 45 minutes to 75 minutes, and if the gradients on the dial are assumed to be accurate without accounting for the time from the equinoxes, incorrect time would result.

A German scientist, Doctor Zinner, has made a catalog of public sundials in Europe, according to Dr. Dolan, and Zinner found over 600 sundials, which might be comparable to the tower clock. In America, the first sundial was built in Salem, MA, and is known as the Endicott dial, named for the builder. Dr. Dolan closed with the notation that even the sundial people have used advanced terminology to describe the product, as a sundial is also called a helio-chronometer.

Dr. Dolan has written a book, *A Choice of Sundials*, published in 1975 by Steven Greene Press of Brattleboro, VT 05301.

---

33. TORONTO

Our Chapter met on June 17th, at the Robert Phillip Museum of Time in Cookstown, Ontario, with 100 or so members and guests dropping in during the course of the afternoon.

Comprised of over 1000 horological items, displayed on 3 floors, this is probably the finest collection in Canada. Our hosts, Mr. and Mrs. Bob Phillip and Bob Jr., split the party into smaller groups, e s c o r t i n g them through the three rooms, describing the historical and technical aspects of many items, and emphasizing any example with special mechanical features. This collection gives a remarkably well balanced picture of the history of timekeeping and of the tools used by the clockmaker.

---

34. OLD DOMINION

Meeting Calendar
Second Sunday — BULLETIN Months

The June 17th meeting was held at the Fort Magruder Inn and Conference Center, Williamsburg, VA.

Our program was "The Swinging Clock," by Roger Holmberg, on loan from National. The Mini-Workshop was "The Jade Clock, How It Was Made Of Jade," by Ted Bhend, also from National.

Bob Draucker reported on the National Convention in Indianapolis. He also gave highlights of the Council meeting and actions taken.

36. HEART OF AMERICA

Meeting Calendar
Second Sunday — BULLETIN Months
Except August

On June 10th 13 members and guests met at the Kansas City, KS, Power and Light Building. Ray Wiggins reported on the recent Great Plains Regional held in Omaha, NE.

The program consisted of a "get acquainted" session where each member and guest introduced himself and described his interests.

37. ALLEGHENY

Meeting Calendar
First Sunday — BULLETIN Months

There was a large turnout for our annual "Point of the Compass" meeting on June 3rd at the Ramada Inn, Washington, PA. A meeting favorite is the members' display of horological items. This time t h e r e was a good display of English clocks and watches.

An unusual member display revealed the damaging effects of a mainspring's explosive force when it suddenly breaks inside a china-cased clock.

Following the buffet and business meeting was a display and talk by Stan Kopia. The display was an epicyclical geared clock with sun and planetary gearing; two hand-made finely detailed miniature grandfather clocks (watches); a skeleton clock followed by a turn-of-the-century electric with fore and aft pendulum motion. The last clock item was an inclined plane. All were hand-made and assembled by Stan. Other items on the table revealed Stan's handicraft in the horological tools and tooling. Genial Stan

Stan Kopia with part of his display of hand-made clocks and tools at Chapter #37's June meeting. (Joe Abrams photo)

explained an electric motor driven tooth cutter he made and used in constructing his clocks.

Stan's talk began with his introduction into the hobby avocation that caused many to walk with him down memory lane. His semi-technical explanations and descriptions of the problems of making his models and tools were easy listening and when one views the exceptional detail, refinements, and workmanship of the pieces, components, and the whole of each completed project, he could not convince us that he is just an electrician. Many questions were obligingly answered.

39. FIRELANDS

Meeting Calendar
First Sunday — BULLETIN Months

On June 3rd, at the Showboat Inn, Huron, OH, there were 33 members present to hear Jack Butchart discuss watch collecting. Ed Hacker presented a slide/tape program from National, "Skeleton Clocks," by Pete Booz and Los Angeles Chapter #56. Woody

Brockhurst explained a clock movement that was reportedly made in South America.

The group held a lively discussion on how to increase membership within the Chapter.

The centerpiece and a small Seth Thomas clock were auctioned off, the proceeds of which will go to the National Building Program.

---

40. RIP VAN WINKLE

Meeting Calendar
November 17, 1984
February 2, 1985

As an example of the tenacity, interest, and enthusiasm among Rip members, over 80 of us found our way to yet one more restaurant for our June 2nd meeting at the New Crossroads Restaurant, Latham, NY. Our search goes on for a permanent meeting place since our former "home" closed as a restaurant and will become a shoe store.

After a busy morning, we had a short business meeting where it was announced that the feature of our summer joint picnic with Chapter #84 will be an auction, proceeds of which will be donated to the NAWCC Museum, Library, and Research Fund.

Alton A. DuBois, Jr., of Hawthorne, NY, a recent new member of Rip, presented a slide program on "Tower Clocks of Albany, NY." His narration stressed many points, starting with the difficulty in getting to the mechanisms to photograph them, not because people didn't want to cooperate, but mainly because people didn't know where the entrance was to get to a given clock. He showed us excellent pictures — a tribute to his perseverance. Unfortunately, many clocks have been electrified, but in some cases, the old works are still there, unused. In the cases where the clocks have been modified and no longer use the original mechanisms, the original mechanisms are deteriorating through neglect. He showed pictures of the Albany City Hall clock, the Home City Savings Bank clock, clocks in several churches in Albany and towns south of the city. There is a message here that

NAWCC Chapters could make a contribution to horology by searching out the tower clocks in their areas and offering advice and support to the town's business or churches in the restoration of their tower clocks. Some of the organizations that have these tower clocks which have been modified and no longer use the original works, might be willing to donate the original works to the NAWCC Museum. This is something that the Museum Committee might be interested in pursuing.

---

43. CREOLE

On July 15th we met at the Covington, LA, High School with 75 members attending. The most discussed business at this meeting was our hosting of the 1985 Regional to be held in March in Metairie, LA. Don Henderson is the Chairman of this Regional.

---

44. KENTUCKY FLORAL CLOCK

Meeting Calendar
Second Sunday — MART Months

An outing at Lake Malone State Park was combined with the July 8th meeting of our Chapter. Those attending enjoyed the interesting clock display and the question and answer session conducted by Budgie Payne.

The members that attended the National in Indianapolis passed on their observations, experiences, views, and opinions to those that didn't attend.

---

47. MENOMONEE VALLEY

Meeting Calendar
Fourth Sunday — January,
March, July, September
Third Sunday — May, November

On May 20th, we held our meeting at the Circle B Recreation Center in Cedarburg, WI.

Various antique watchmaker's tools were exhibited by Rudy Pauers. Lee Eisenberg displayed his restored

French Statue Classic clock, made of solid brass, circa 1844-1849.

The slide/tape program from National, "What To Look For In Buying A Watch," by Joe Shaffer and Bill Meggers, instructed us on what to be aware of when looking at the cases and movements of pocket and wristwatches.

---

48. KING COTTON

Meeting Calendar
Second Saturday — MART Months

The 28 members and guests who attended our July 14th meeting at the Pink Palace Museum in Memphis, TN, were treated to an unusual display of clocks, watches, and horological items. President Brimm announced a new program directed toward the new collectors to help them enlarge their collections by having Chapter members bring items they no longer collected, wanted, or had not repaired, and making these items available at original cost. Those items not purchased by newer collectors were then to be offered to other members for any price

Two unusual 8-day Junghans timepieces brought for Chapter #48's "new member" sale by Tommy Garstang.

agreed on, with any excess over cost to be donated to the Museum Expansion Fund. Such items were brought by Ed Hull, Marvin Edwards, Tommy Garstang, Glen Alexander, and Jack Brimm. The idea will be continued at future meetings.

Our program, presented by President Brimm, was on slides of the National Convention at Indianapolis. Vice-President Rel Morgan then presented a Certificate of Appreciation to member Marvin Edwards. This award was announced at Indianapolis.

Phil Wallace brought a pivot polisher made for him by Bob Oakley; Jim Scoggins brought an unusual Junghans desk clock; Tommy Garstang brought two large Junghans wall clocks; and Dr. Davis Brown brought a Brewster & Ingrahams "Venetian" 30-hour clock with the original brass springs. Rel Morgan had the hit of the show with his Asa Munger model Hotchkiss & Benedict weight clock. This clock was one of the models made by New York State prisoners about 1835-36.

Rel Morgan shows his New York prisoner-made Asa Munger model Hotchkiss and Benedict clock to fellow Chapter #48 members.

---

50. PUGET SOUND

Meeting Calendar
Second Saturday or Sunday —
Each Month

On June 12th we met at the home of Mr. and Mrs. Reichel, Kent, WA. Members brought watches and clocks for exhibiting, and Bob Reichel showed his Forestville Manufacturing Co., J. C. Brown Acorn clock.

Forestville Clock Manufacturing Co., J. C. Brown Enterprise, "The Acorn": a glass door from his Acorn clock is shown by Bob Reichel (left), of Chapter #50, to Del Lewis. Bob had the movement for 10 years. He recently obtained the original case from a member in Cuddebachville, NY. The tablet (reverse painting on glass) is original, only the branches and acorn finish need replacing.

55. CENTRAL NEW YORK

Meeting Calendar
November 4, 1984

On June 3rd, 122 members and guests gathered at the Holiday Inn, Courtland, NY. Russ Oechsle gave a progress report on our Regional scheduled for August.

Maxwell Schaller gave a workshop on "Cuckoo Clocks and Their Repair," and Joel Warren gave a wood carving demonstration. For the ladies, we had a discussion on cloth stenciling.

Following our business meeting we saw the program from National, "Ansonia and Its Clocks," by Marjorie and Charles Partridge.

57. OZARK

Our May 20th meeting was held at the Ramada Inn, Fayetteville, AR, with all present Chapter Officers re-elected to another year of service. Our program, on clock restoration, was conducted by Mike Wisdom. This has been covered many times before, but never from this unique viewpoint. Mike restores clocks for a living, so time used on their restoration must be kept to a minimum. He has developed many time-saving methods. He also touched on general public preferences in case finishes, dial tones, hands, etc., making many Ozark collectors aware that our preferences are sometimes at variance with the ideal as seen by the public. All members agreed that it would have been difficult not to have picked up useful information from this presentation.

58. GREAT PLAINS

Meeting Calendar
Second Sunday — MART Months

The annual Great Plains Regional was held in Omaha, NE, May 18-20, with Chapter #91 as co-host.

Special programs were: Samuel Jennings, "The Evolution of Eli Terry's Shelf Clock"; Marguerite Utiger, "The Bertrand Clock"; and Stan McElvain, "Central Iowa Clocks." All were very exceptional and educational programs.

Special thanks to Bernie Edwards, National Secretary, for being guest speaker at the banquet.

*

Ray Pike, Chapter #58's
July program speaker.

There were 46 members and guests in attendance at the July 8th meeting held at the Short Stop Restaurant in Omaha, NE.

Ray Pike gave a talk on clock repair hints including don'ts for beginners. Some of the don'ts covered were: spray lube for clocks, soldering on the plates, tightening holes in plates with punches instead of bushings, etc. The underlying theme of his talk was to keep the movements as close to the original shape and design as possible and not to ruin them for future collectors.

The membership was saddened by the sudden death of Donald Johansen in May. Don was a charter member who always took a very active part in all proceedings.

Samuel Jennings
presenting his program at
the Great Plains Regional
hosted by Chapter #58.

59. SAN DIEGO COUNTY

Meeting Calendar
Second Saturday — Each Month

The Southwest California Regional took place May 10-13 at the Scottish Rite Center, San Diego, CA. This year we had a breakfast Saturday morning rather than a Saturday evening banquet. The National President, Gene Bagwell, was our speaker.

We were very fortunate to have three distinguished gentlemen in the field of horology present our programs. They were: Chipman Ela, "Identification of B a n j o Clocks"; Ward Francillon, "The Wooden-Works Mantel Clock"; and Bill Meggers, "Some Guidelines for B e g i n n i n g Watch Collectors."

*

On June 9th 56 members and guests met at the same location. Show & Tell included a New Haven cottage clock; a French carved mahogany hanger cartel clock, which has a second dial on the back operated by extra gears; a battery-plate clock; a Waterbury carriage clock; an unusual device — an old-fashioned two-button l i g h t switch which could be turned off by means of the alarm function of a clock mechanism; a clock housed in a case made from a German field artillery shell, with an identifying plate indicating that there might have been quite a few such clocks created; an antique music box with 4 selectable tunes (so old that nobody recognized the names); an old travel clock and the original carrying case; a Gilbert bim-bam wall clock; and a 15-jewel solid b r a s s 8-day clock by Seth Thomas.

The program for the evening was the slide/tape from National, "American Wall Hanging Seconds Beat Regulators," by Dorothy & Glenn Marsh.

---

61. ROCKET CITY REGULATORS

Meeting Calendar
Second Saturday — Each Month

Our Chapter meeting was held at Shoney's Restaurant on June 16th with 21 members attending. Reports of the National Convention were given. Praise was given for the recent BULLETIN Supplement on American watchmaking, by Michael C. Harrold. All agreed that this is an excellent piece of work and worthy of commendation. The program, from National, presented by Ken Easter, was "The Rise & Fall of the Vienna Regulator," by Pete Booz. We enjoyed the excellent photography.

Recognition was given to James W. Foster and Cecil Rayburn for honors received from National. These two have contributed significantly to the activities of the local Chapters and the National organization.

---

63. SUNFLOWER CLOCK WATCHERS

Meeting Calendar
First Friday — Each Month

Our Chapter meeting of June 1st was held at the Wichita, KS, Area Vocational-Technical School Library. The program was presented by President Kenneth Thompson and Jerry Bamesberger on the Friends University tower clock. The E. Howard 4-dial clock was a gift to the University, a Quaker institution located in Wichita, by the senior class of 1931. The movement is weight-driven, with electric wind, dead-beat escapement model. A similar model was installed in Wichita's Sedgwick County Courthouse in 1890 — a l t h o u g h not electrically wound. Ken and Jerry made an adventure out of their trip up in the tower and brought back numerous photographs of the clock movement showing its present worn, but operating, dirty condition, as well as the poor environment in which it must operate. A very good program, indeed.

*

Our July 6th meeting, held at the same location, was called to order by President Kenneth Thompson. Ursula Metsker presented Kenneth Thompson with a Presidential Citation award received from National for Chapter work.

Dale White, our Program Chairman,

presented a program on "Hunter Case" watches. He displayed and discussed a wide variety of case styles and movements, including some with box hinges, very detailed engraving, cases of gold and coin silver, old key wind movements, and one with a Braille dial. It was a very informative program. Our Show & Tell brought out a good selection of clocks, watches, and miscellaneous, including Stacy Wood's new book on the clocks in the NAWCC Museum. The book, entitled *The Wonderful World of Time*, is very interesting and is available from National. Also for sale at the meeting was a new book published by Chapter #120 on horological statues.

67. SAGINAW VALLEY

Meeting Calendar
Last Sunday — MART Months

On May 20th, a joint meeting of our Chapter and Chapter #101 was held at Long's Restaurant in Lansing, MI, with approximately 60 members and guests attending. Following dinner a fine slide program was presented by guest speaker Bill Porter on tower clocks. The program included pictures of different tower clock movements as well as different tower clock towers. Bill also showed many slides of his own tower clock collection.

69. ORANGE COUNTY

Meeting Calendar
First Friday — Each Month

Our June 1st meeting, held at the Ebell Club in Santa Ana, CA, was attended by 100 members and guests. The results of the election of Officers are: M. A. Saiben, President; and James H. Espy, Secretary.

Retiring President Jim Krause gave the State of the Chapter message, and we were pleased to learn our membership is holding at 200.

Show & Tell was for recently acquired horological items, with prizes won by Bud Saiben, Lawrence Dougherty, and Mr. McAlister. Door prizes

were won by Lawrence Dougherty, Bill Clark, and Ed Thouvenin.

Our program from National was, "The Jade Clock, How It Was Made Of Jade," by Ted Bhend.

72. FIRST AUSTRALIAN

Meeting Calendar
First Sunday — BULLETIN Months
Except Second Sunday in October

The June 3rd meeting, held in Wentworthville, A u s t r a l i a , took on a slightly different format, starting with a slide show. These slides reviewed the Chapter's great clock exhibitions at Parramatta in 1977 and 1982. The purpose of this nostalgia was to enthuse members to partake in yet another Chapter exhibition at Wentworthville in October of this year. Plans were made to coordinate the activities with the Annual Holroyd Family Festival.

Question Time analyzed some fine clocks and later a LOGITECH quartz beat monitor for fast clock regulation. Library and afternoon tea concluded a busy day.

78. ELECTRICAL HOROLOGY SOCIETY

The annual summer meeting of the New York/New Jersey area members of the EHS was graciously hosted at the home of Mr. & Mrs. Alan Marx on June 24th. To make it easier for members to meet and for other NAWCC collectors to be exposed to electrical horology, our Vice-President, Marty Swetsky, will try to arrange meetings during the various Regionals throughout the country. We are a Chapter with an international membership held together by our common interest and the Journal of the Electrical Horology Society, published six times per year. Membership is open to all NAWCC members in good standing (see back of BULLETIN for Secretary's name). After the short business meeting, the group discussed various electrical clocks which were brought for exhibit.

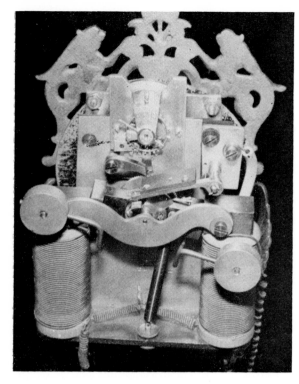

A Moller electro-magnetically rewound remontoire balance wheel movement of German manufacture, ca. 1920, brought for exhibition at #78's meeting.
(M. Feldman photo)

89. MAINE

On June 21st we met in Freeport, ME, at the Harrasseeket Grange Hall with more than 60 members and guests attending. Among the guests was Raymond I. Booth, Jr., a member of Chapter #68.

Paul Bennett, Carol Morse, and Cal Morgan were appointed members of the Nominating Committee, Bill Eberly was appointed to the position of Chapter representative to assist in raising money for the Campaign for the NAWCC Museum & Research Center. Cal Morgan volunteered to help.

The proposed repair of George Bush's Japanese clock was again discussed. As yet we have not seen Mr. Bush or his clock, but President Rehler has had recent correspondence with him and the clock is scheduled to receive treatment soon.

93. SOUTH JERSEY

Meeting Calendar
Third Sunday — Each Month
Except July, August

The July 1st meeting was our 3rd annual picnic held at the Lacey Township, NJ, Elks Club. There were 81 members and guests attending the day-long affair. In addition to the new members joining that day, we had a number of guests attending from our sister Chapter #25 in north Jersey.

Our President, Jack Rubin, was the auctioneer at the lively, successful auction. Those present enjoyed the many horological items on display as well as the discussions provided.

94. DE ANZA

Meeting Calendar
First Sunday — BULLETIN Months
Except August

The June 3rd meeting was held at the McKinnon School, San Jose, CA. All of the $500 pledge to the National Museum was raised at this meeting.

We were saddened by the news of the death of one of our members, Willard LeCroy, after a lengthy illness.

Roger Holmberg presented, in person, his NAWCC program on Swinging Pendulum Clocks, with a large number of beautiful slides. It was very interesting and informative.

---

98. CALOOSA

Meeting Calendar
First Saturday — Each Month
Except July, August, September

The June 2nd meeting, held at the Hatchcover Restaurant, Ft. Myers, FL, was attended by 29 members and 1 guest. We again had a nice representation of horological items. Our educational presentation consisted of a slide /tape program from National, "Carriage Clocks," by O. B. Frye and Chapter #46.

---

99. PALM BEACHES OF FLORIDA

Meeting Calendar
Fourth Sunday — Each Month
Except July, August

The June 24th meeting, held at the Royal Palm Clubhouse, Boynton Beach, FL, was attended by 42 members and guests. Ben Bollinger, introduced by President Ozzie Nelson, gave a slide presentation on the recent National Convention held at Indianapolis, IN. Our Chapter won the NAWCC Presidential Award for the 3rd year in a row. Two of our members, Gerhard Hutter and Len Rutlin, won NAWCC awards. Our guest speaker, from the Allstate Insurance Co., talked about fine arts insurance on clocks and watches. Tom Colandrea spoke on ships' clocks, and Ed Malette gave a short talk on Waltham and repeater watches.

---

101. WESTERN MICHIGAN

Meeting Calendar
Third Sunday — BULLETIN Months
Except First Sunday in December

Our Chapter met with Chapter #67 for a joint meeting held May 20th at Long's Restaurant in Lansing, MI, with 64 members and guests present. Bob Arnold from Saginaw Valley introduced speaker Bill Porter. Bill spoke on Tower Clocks and illustrated his talk with several slides of tower clocks in his personal collection.

---

107. DIABLO VALLEY

Meeting Calendar
Second Sunday — BULLETIN Months

Our June 10th meeting, held at the Pleasant Hill, CA, Recreation Center, was well attended. We were treated to an excellent slide presentation and discussion on American Clocks by our eminent member, Dorothy Glenk. Her programs are always well received because of her good slides and thorough knowledge.

---

114. BROOKLYN

Meeting Calendar
November 26, 1984
December 17, 1984

The June 18th meeting, held at Collaro's Restaurant, honored our outgoing President, Dominick Clemente, who was presented a set of Roy Ehrhardt's books. Rochelle Gaenger, President of Chapter #88, and a member of the Awards Committee, presented the Chapter with a Presidential Citation from National. Dan Gaenger, President of Chapter #2, spoke to us about participation in the New York Regional.

A motion to donate $100 to the National Building Fund was passed and a check was drawn up.

*

At the June 25th meeting, held at the Atlantic Liberty Savings and Loan Association, the installation of new Officers was held: Arthur L. Winakor, President; Martin Swetsky, Vice-President; John Munnelly, Secretary; and Nils Nelson, Treasurer.

were pictures of Harrison's 4 chronometers, preserved at Greenwich, on which he worked a lifetime. His designs led to accurate timekeeping, enabling ships to navigate more precisely, rather than having to guess at their locations.

116. SANTA ANITA

Meeting Calendar
Second Wednesday — Each Month

On June 13th we met at the Acadia, CA, Elks Lodge. Lloyd Porter presented the slide program from National, "Western Regional Exhibit at San Mateo," by Fred Bausch and Lloyd Porter. The slides had been beautifully photographed by Jack Barrow of our Chapter. The Show & Tell portion of the meeting was on the topic, Anything You Got at a Regional, and that theme touched almost everyone!

*

Lloyd Porter presided over the July meeting, held at the same location, as a stand-in for President Hap Holladay who is off on an extended horological vacation in Europe. Lloyd showed the program, "Clocks and Watches of European Museums," by Dr. H. P. Holladay and Lloyd Porter. Outstanding

117. RIO GRANDE

Meeting Calendar
Second Saturday — MART Months

The July 14th meeting was held at the home of Rollo Gurss, El Paso, TX, located on one of the higher mountains surrounding the city. There were 29 members and guests present.

The highlight of the meeting was the installation of Officers at the covered dish dinner which has traditionally become an annual event at the end of the fiscal year.

The following Officers were installed: Charles Gates, President and Program Chairman; John Novitski, Vice-President; Edgar Surface, Secretary-Treasurer; and Arne Hansen, Membership Chairman.

Outgoing President Ed Bush was presented with a plaque thanking him for serving as our President for the past 3 years.

120. HOROLOGICAL ART

Meeting Calendar
November 2-3, 1984
June 20-23, 1985

Our annual meeting was held June 7th at the National Convention in Indianapolis, IN. The program was "Miniature Clocks" and was presented by Chapter member Lloyd Porter. The program, available from National, pictures and describes the cases and movements of a number of miniature clocks (some only two inches high) from the collection of Lloyd and his late wife, Jane.

President Rochelle Gaenger announced that the booklet on clockmaker/watchmaker figurines had been completed and is now available for sale. The booklet pictures items from the collections of several Chapter

Gigi Holladay, Vice-President of Chapter #116, with NAWCC President Gene Bagwell.

members. A percentage of the sale price of each book will be donated to the NAWCC Museum Building Fund.

Our Chapter Bylaws require that we have two meetings each year, the annual meeting held in conjunction with the National Convention, and a second meeting held in conjunction with a scheduled Regional meeting. As it is impossible for all members to attend both or sometimes even one of these meetings, the Chapter has decided to schedule an informal meeting and program at each Regional. The President will appoint a Chapter member in a particular Regional area to arrange and handle the meeting. When possible, a Chapter Officer will attend. It is hoped that this will further stimulate interest in the Chapter for our members and prospective members. We urge all non-Chapter members who are collectors of horological art (inanimates, figurines, prints, etc.) to participate in these meetings and join the Chapter.

The next scheduled business meeting will be held in conjunction with the Mid-Eastern Regional on November 2-3, 1984, in Charlotte, NC.

---

123. PRESCOTT HIGH TIMERS

Meeting Calendar
November 11, 1984
January 13, 1985

Our July 8th meeting was held at the home of Jim and Doris Inman in Oak Creek Canyon, AZ. The program was a follow-up to our last side program from National on the Dr. Sobek collection of Vienna Regulators. This time, members John Carlson and Ken Law described the design of the movements and the case construction details which have made Vienna Regulators so valued and sought after.

John Carlson (left) explains the design details of a 3-weight Vienna Regulator movement. Ken Law shows a Biedermeier period Regulator case to the members of Chapter #123.

126. WESTERN CAROLINAS

Meeting Calendar
November 13, 1984
January 8, 1985

Our July 10th meeting was held at the Northwestern Bank in Hendersonville, NC. Chapter President Phil Gilbert displayed the NAWCC Presidential Citation received at the National Convention. The citation was given to the Chapter by NAWCC President Bagwell for our work in restoring the street clock on Main Street in Hendersonville.

The membership voted to contribute $100 to the National Museum Fund. This amount may not seem a great deal but it represents 40% of our treasury. Virge Kenerson, Chapter Museum Fund Chairman, accepted the check and pointed out that even though the Chapter made a contribution, each member should contribute on his own.

Member T. A. Brawley gave a short talk on the National Convention in Indianapolis, IN, for those unable to attend.

Our speaker was member John Saby, who gave an excellent talk on identifying wooden works. This was done by using Lester Beers' program, "Wooden Works and Their Differences," plus additional slides and Snowden Taylor's Part II of the December, 1982, BULLETIN on wooden works. John presented a hand-out to the members showing the key areas to check for a quick identification system. He also brought many movements for a hands-on examination, and a few members brought examples for identification.

---

129. SUNDIAL

Meeting Calendar
Third Thursday — Each Month

On June 21st we met at Beefmasters, Ft. Walton Beach, FL. Nomination Chairman Eugene Hammer presented the slate of Officers for the 1984-85 year. As there were no nominations from the floor, the following were elected: President, Eugene Hammer; Vice-President and Program Chairman, James Brown; Historian-Photographer, Al Dykes; Secretary, Peggy Maselowitch; and Treasurer, Wilson Suggs.

The program, presented by Tom Blizzard and Hilton Earle, was a presentation from National, "Behind the Dial #1," by George A. Peterson.

CHAPTER OFFICERS

(This listing is being printed to help National members contact Chapter officials.)

1. PHILADELPHIA
President Cy Felheimer, 524 Fern Ave., Westmont, NJ 08108
Secretary Mrs. Cecelia Sweisford, 705 Walnut St., Royersford, PA 19468
2. NEW YORK
President Daniel J. Gaenger, 18 School St., E. Williston, NY 11596
Secretary Mrs. Anne M. Drucker, 22 Cranberry Ln., Plainview, NY 11803
3. CHICAGOLAND
President Ted Kamish, 3018 W. Montrose Ave., Chicago, IL 60618
Secretary Gene Lehman, 228 E. Hicks Pl., Palatine, IL 60067
4. SOUTHERN CALIFORNIA
President Dr. Bengt E. Honning, 3736 Atlantic Ave. Ste. 4, Long Beach, CA 90807
Secretary Mrs. Dorothy Severns, 6910 Lime Ave., Long Beach, CA 90805
5. SAN FRANCISCO — DR. W. BARCLAY STEPHENS MEMORIAL
President Seth Finkelstein, 2311 Chanticleer Ave., Santa Cruz, CA 95062
Secretary C. F. Kroeger, 1999 Ashby Ave., Berkeley, CA 94703
6. GREAT LAKES
President George Hedges, 5711 Pebbleshire Rd., Birmingham, MI 48010
Secretary Mrs. Peggy Timlin, 5846 Kenilworth, Dearborn, MI 48126
7. HEADQUARTERS — EARL T. STRICKLER MEMORIAL
President Paul J. Kuhn, R.D. 1, Box 191-D, Hershey, PA 17033
Secretary Barry Gibbons, P.O. Box 243, Lancaster, PA 17603
8. NEW ENGLAND
President Wiliam F. Hofmann, Jr., 5 Fieldmont Rd., Belmont, MA 02178
Secretary Donald F. Procko, 84 Hazelmere Rd., New Britain, CT 06053

9. TOKYO, JAPAN
President Sumio Hirai, Hirai Tokeiten 5-2-4 Ueno, Taito-Ku, Tokyo 110, Japan
Secretary Yukichi Ozawa, 2-28-11-307 Honcho, Nakano-Ku, Tokyo, Japan
10. OHIO VALLEY
President Mark C. Fulmer, 1824 3rd St. S.E., Canton, OH 44707
Secretary Edmund H. Anthon, Jr., 30 Woolf Ave., Akron, OH 44312
11. MARYLAND
President Thomas F. Mostyn, 2700 Gibbons Ave., Baltimore, MD 21214
Secretary Mrs. Deanne G. Mostyn, 2700 Gibbons Ave., Baltimore, MD 21214
12. WASHINGTON, DC
President Kathleen H. Pritchard, 9201 Laurel Oak Dr., Bethesda, MD 20817
Secretary Paul D. Simpson, 2016 Colebrook Dr., Temple Hills, MD 20748
13. WESTERN NEW YORK
President Charles F. Roeser, 500 S. Transit St., Lockport, NY 14094
Secretary Paul Pietrzak, 7526 Valley Circle Ln., Hamburg, NY 14075
14. ST. LOUIS, MO
President Robert E. Webb, 594 Blanche Dr., St. Charles, MO 63301
Secretary Gus Weinstock, P.O. Box 8307, Olivette, MO 63132
15. SOUTHWESTERN
President Hugh C. Overton, Jr., 2442 Walnut Ridge St., Dallas, TX 75229
Secretary Mrs. Dovie Mayes, 4208 Boca Bay, Dallas, TX 75234
16. DIXIE
President Herbert C. Cary, 902 Shadow Ln., Mt. Juliet, TN 37122
Secretary Mrs. Gwen Blanton, 811 Windmere Dr., Lebanon, TN 37087
17. CAROLINA
President Mrs. Bryte R. Walker, 2522 Roswell Ave., Charlotte, NC 28209
Secretary Mrs. Ruth Ann Dunnuck, 6 Wakerobin Ct., Greensboro, NC 27407
18. INDIANA
President Dr. Bobby G. Bryant, 1120 S. 22nd, Lafayette, IN 47905
Secretary William S. Stoddard, 539 E. 57th St., Indianapolis, IN 46220
19. FLORIDA SUNTIME
President D. E. Timmons, Jr., P.O. Box 8765, Tampa, FL 33674
Secretary Mrs. Carole C. Mayer, 144 E. Stuart Ave., Lake Wales, FL 33853
20. MINNESOTA — OSCAR T. LANG MEMORIAL
President William L. Gable, 4207 13th Ave. S., Minneapolis, MN 55407
Secretary James J. Winkels, 4725 Emerson Ave. S., Minneapolis, MN 55409
21. COLORADO
President Clyde A. Maxey, 3724 S. Taft Hill Rd., Ft. Collins, CO 80526
Secretary Roger L. Dankert, 1558 S. Jamaica St., Aurora, CO 80012
22. OLD TIMERS
President Henry B. Fried, 69-53 180th St., Flushing, NY 11365
Secretary Mrs. Rose P. Brandt, Star Route, Ridge Rd., Box 65, Glens Falls, NY 12801
23. BUCKEYE
President Ned E. Weymouth, 311 Wiltshire Blvd., Dayton, OH 45419
Secretary D. L. Goss, 4 Beverly Pl., Dayton, OH 45419
24. ATLANTA
President Col. J. Edgar Morris, 2793 Woodland Park Dr. N.E., Atlanta, GA 30345
Secretary Conrad G. Flowers, 1297 Plymouth Dr., Lilburn, GA 30247
25. NEW JERSEY
President Mrs. Arlene Bizlewicz, P.O. Box 209, Chester, NJ 07930
Secretary Steven G. Conover, 180 Elizabeth Ave., Iselin, NJ 08830
26. GEORGE E. LEE — MICHIANA
President John Lantz, 2803 Roscommon Dr., Fort Wayne, IN 46805
Secretary Richard Tjarks, 809 S. Union St., Lagrange, IN 46761
27. DELAWARE
President Henry Bouchelle, 1725 Delaware Ave., Wilmington, DE 19806
Secretary David B. Maguire, 9 Edgemont Rd., Newark, DE 19711
28. LAKE ERIE
President Mark A. Carpenter, 2644 River Rd., Willoughby Hills, OH 44094
Secretary Stanley J. Kaufman, 829 Homewood Dr., Painesville, OH 44077
29. IOWA-ILLINOIS
President Charles R. Cline, Box 805, Bettendorf, IA 52722
Secretary Warren E. Lange, 717 Downey Dr., Princeton, IL 61356
30. CHEROKEE
President Ronald G. Starnes, 7315 E. 24th St., Tulsa, OK 74129
Secretary Mary Ann Stanton, 1320 S. Winston, Tulsa, OK 74112
31. PACIFIC-NORTHWEST
President Robert A. Higgins, Rt. #3, Box 167, Sherwood, OR 97140
Secretary Robert K. Hughes, P.O. Box 13503, Portland, OR 97213
32. SHENANDOAH VALLEY OF VIRGINIA
President Fred Horton, 4024 Oakland Blvd. N.W., Roanoke, VA 24012
Secretary Mrs. Loetta W. Horton, 4024 Oakland Blvd. N.W., Roanoke, VA 24012
33. TORONTO
President J. N. Turnbull, 245 Golfdale Rd., Toronto, Ont., Canada M4N 2C2
Secretary John N. Burke, 54 Robertsfield Cres., Scarboro, Ont., Canada M1R 2X3

34. OLD DOMINION
President   James E. Duckworth, 5904 Old Orchard Rd., Richmond, VA 23227
Secretary   Mrs. Judy T. Draucker, 1232 Bell Creek Rd., Mechanicsville, VA 23111
35. KENTUCKY BLUE-GRASS
President   Philip Balcomb, 104 Geneva Dr., Tell City, IN 47586
Secretary   Mrs. Bernita R. Buschermohle, 4200 Old Heady Rd., Jeffersontown, KY 40299
36. HEART OF AMERICA
President   Delbert W. Herrmann, 5839 Perry Ln., Merriam, KS 66203
Secretary   Roger J. Schroeder, 4111 W. 98th St., Overland Park, KS 66207
37. ALLEGHENY
President   John A. Petitto, 1021 Old Gate Rd., Pittsburgh, PA 15235
Secretary   Joseph J. Abrams, 806 Belmont Rd., Butler, PA 16001
38. MAUMEE VALLEY
President   Robert J. Reifert, 2921 Emmick Dr., Toledo, OH 43606
Secretary   Mrs. Janet A. Reifert, 2921 Emmick Dr., Toledo, OH 43606
39. FIRELANDS
President   Donald S. Bass, 1511 E. Perkins Ave., Sandusky, OH 44870
Secretary   Mort A. Plato, 195 S. Leavitt Rd., Amherst, OH 44001
40. RIP VAN WINKLE
President   Raymond W. Fischer, 71 Sunnyside Dr., Dalton, MA 01226
Secretary   Mrs. Albert E. Whiton, 100 E. Housatonic St., Pittsfield, MA 01201
41. MAGNOLIA
President   Andy D. Palmer, Rt. 3, Box 301-A, Florence, MS 39073
Secretary   John H. McDonald, Jr., P.O. Box 683, Clinton, MS 39056
42. TENNESSEE VALLEY
President   Kermit Duckett, 3404 Timberlake Rd., Knoxville, TN 37920
Secretary   Ms. Paula Gammell, 7442 Oak Ridge Hwy., Knoxville, TN 37931
43. CREOLE
President   Jim H. Bruce, 7009 Colonial Pl., Denham Springs, LA 70726
Secretary   Simon A. LaSalle, 509 Ridgelake Dr., Metairie, LA 70001
44. KENTUCKY FLORAL CLOCK
President   Greg Bates, 5750 Graham Ln., Owensboro, KY 42301
Secretary   Roby Robertson, 1919 Eaton Ave., Owensboro, KY 42301
45. ARK-LA-TEX
President   W. Frank Stawasz, Jr., 8347 Kelly Ln., Shreveport, LA 71129
Secretary   Mrs. Susan M. Stawasz, 8347 Kelly Ln., Shreveport, LA 71129
46. KEYWINDERS OF ARIZONA
President   Dr. Hugh G. Wales, 2021 S. La Rosa Dr., Tempe, AZ 85282
Secretary   William D. Sonik, P.O. Box 1853, Sun City, AZ 85372
47. MENOMONEE VALLEY
President   Donald Brown, 515 Oakwood Dr., Thiensville, WI 53092
Secretary   Mrs. Irene Temke, 1920 S. 72nd St., W. Allis, WI 53219
48. KING COTTON
President   W. L. (Jack) Brimm, Jr., 4834 Welchshire Ave., Memphis, TN 38117
Secretary   Mrs. Joe Ann Brimm, 4834 Welchshire Ave., Memphis, TN 38117
49. TRI-STATE — H. C. SHANHOLTZ MEMORIAL
President   Michael R. Cline, 1531 Dixie St., Charleston, WV 25311
Secretary   Ronald A. Baehl, 1989 Parkwood Rd., Charleston, WV 25314
50. PUGET SOUND
President   Ralph E. Peel, 2762 Northlake Way N.W., Bremerton, WA 98312
Secretary   Mrs. Kay Anderson, 7925 206th St. S.E., Snohomish, WA 98290
51. MID-MISSOURI
President   Dr. Harry A. Knauff, 6511 W. 49th St., Mission, KS 66202
Secretary   Ltc. Jere A. DeVilbiss, Rt. 4, Fox Ln., Columbia, MO 65201
52. LOS PADRES
President   Burton J. Krieger, 885 Comanche Ave., Santa Maria, CA 93455
Secretary   Mrs. Frances M. Tolly, 1246 Tree Ln., Oxnard, CA 93033
53. INLAND EMPIRE
President   Laurence E. Pearson, 2292 Granite Dr., Walla Walla, WA 99362
Secretary   Mrs. Elizabeth G. Lord, S.W. 1145 Marcel St., Pullman, WA 99163
54. ALABAMA
President   Paul Hopkins, 2117 Millwood Rd., Birmingham, AL 35243
Secretary   Mrs. David L. McLeroy, P.O. Box 1432, Columbiana, AL 35051
55. CENTRAL NEW YORK
President   Robert J. Catterfeld, 56 Cayuga St., Homer, NY 13077
Secretary   Mrs. Patricia E. Catterfeld, 56 Cayuga St., Homer, NY 13077
56. LOS ANGELES
President   Robert Seitz, 22537 Flamingo St., Woodland Hills, CA 91364
Secretary   Paul E. Hackamack, 967 Lindencliff St., Torrance, CA 90502
57. OZARK
President   Dr. John K. Day, 1834 Wheeler, Fayetteville, AR 72701
Secretary   J. C. Allen, P.O. Box 56, Carthage, MO 64836
58. GREAT PLAINS
President   Ray Pike, III, 1905 Collins Dr., Bellevue, NE 68005
Secretary   Mike McNichols, 119 S. 53rd St., Omaha, NE 68123

59. SAN DIEGO COUNTY
President   Mrs. Loah L. Horton, 13525 Maryearl Ct., Poway, CA 92064
Secretary   Arnie P. Lacombe, 7914 Port Royal Dr., San Diego, CA 92126
60. FLORIDA GOLD COAST
President   Robert G. Leavitt, 11601 S.W. 82nd Ave., Miami, FL 33156
Secretary   Mrs. Mary Kozak, 1960 N.E. 124th St., N. Miami, FL 33181
61. ROCKET CITY REGULATORS
President   James O. Richeson, 611 Red Lane Rd., Birmingham, AL 35215
Secretary   Forrest W. Streeter, 718 Gillespie Rd., Madison, AL 35758
62. ARKANSAS RAZORBACK
President   James R. Carlisle, 5112 Loetscher Ln., Little Rock, AR 72209
Secretary   Pete M. Cronos, III, 15 Ross Cir., Jacksonville, AR 72076
63. SUNFLOWER CLOCK WATCHERS
President   Kenneth Thompson, 6618 E. 10th, Wichita, KS 67206
Secretary   James W. Shaw, Jr., P.O. Box 1646, Hutchinson, KS 67504
64. PRAIRIE WINDERS
President   Elmer L. Steinle, 1224 Brooks, Russell, KS 67665
Secretary   Ivan Simmonds, 218 W. Court, Smith Center, KS 66967
65. SIERRA-NEVADA
President   Luther A. Boller, 3673 Green Acre Dr., Carson, NV 89701
Secretary   L. Robert McCune, Box 5373, Concord, CA 94524
66. CENTRAL ILLINOIS
President   Dr. James H. Jacobsen, 526 E. Carroll St., Macomb, IL, 61455
Secretary   Leland Koerner, Rt. 1, Chatsworth, IL 60921
67. SAGINAW VALLEY
President   Donald Ingebrigtson, 1026 Balfour, Midland, MI 48640
Secretary   Michael Nestell, 9265 Warnick, Frankenmuth, MI 48734
68. JEAN RIBAULT
President   Charles R. Way, 5816 Paradise Ln., Orlando, FL 32808
Secretary   Peter Recourt, 7620 Saddle Rd., Jacksonville, FL 32205
69. ORANGE COUNTY
President   M. A. Saiben, 18072 Santa Clara Ave., Santa Ana, CA 92705
Secretary   James H. Espy, 17131 El Cajon, Yorba Linda, CA 92686
70. MONTEREY BAY
President   Seth Finkelstein, 2311 Chanticleer Ave., Santa Cruz, CA 95062
Secretary   Mrs. Nancy Turner, 18569 Eucalyptus Dr., Los Gatos, CA 95030
71. SACRAMENTO VALLEY
President   Louis E. Gentry, 5105 Olean St., Fair Oaks, CA 95628
Secretary   Thomas Allen Burton, 831 Columbia Dr., Sacramento, CA 95825
72. FIRST AUSTRALIAN
President   Douglas Minty, 69 Railway St., Wentworthville, N.S.W., 2145, Australia
Secretary   Howard W. Bate, 15 Buckland Ave., Carlinford, N.S.W., 2118, Australia
73. HIGH DESERT
President   Edward H. Lyman, 1213 N. Calvert Blvd., Ridgecrest, CA 93555
Secretary   Mrs. Nancie Loscar, 746 Upjohn Rd., Ridgecrest, CA 93555
74. SOONER TIME COLLECTORS
President   Paul H. Vrooman, 1805 N.W. 56 Terr., Oklahoma City, OK 73118
Secretary   Robert B. Cunningham, 5932 Seminole Rd., Oklahoma City, OK 73132
75. SAN FERNANDO VALLEY
President   Howard J. Banta, 18631 Vincennes St., Northridge, CA 91324
Secretary   James Gilmore, 2909 Raleigh Pl., Thousand Oaks, CA 91360
76. TIMEKEEPERS
President   Vincent D'Addarie, 162 Woodlawn Rd., Warminster, PA 18974
Secretary   Dr. Harold W. Stetson, 222 N. Chancellor St., Newtown, PA 18940
77. LITTLE EGYPT
President   Dallas McClurken, 802 Dogwood Ln., Marion, IL 62959
Secretary   Samuel W. Jennings, Rt. 1, Box 135, Murphysboro, IL 62966
78. ELECTRICAL HOROLOGY SOCIETY
President   Martin C. Feldman, 620 Reiss Pl., Bronx, NY 10467
Secretary   Charles W. Roth, 2 Circle Ln., Roslyn Heights, NY 11577
79. ENDLESS MOUNTAINS
President
Secretary
80. FIVE STATE COLLECTORS
President   Gary E. Markel, 3214 21st, Lubbock, TX 79410
Secretary   Mrs. Esther Wallace, 1005 Borger St., Plainview, TX 79072
81. ARROWHEAD
President   T. Bruce Clarke, 1351 N. Helen Ave., Ontario, CA 91762
Secretary   Ira W. Leonard, 5620 Mountain View Ave., Riverside, CA 92504
82. ADIRONDACK
President   Merrill D. Dye, 7 Northern Blvd., Hagaman, NY 12086
Secretary   Mrs. Loretta M. Casscles, 45 Pearl St., Hudson Falls, NY 12839
83. PEACE PIPE
President   Jerry L. Hays, 6562 Monument, Portage, IN 46368
Secretary   Elliott Y. Spearin, 312 Holton Ridge, Crown Point, IN 46307

84. MID-HUDSON
President Robert M. Otto, 96 W. Van Ness St., Newburgh, NY 12550
Secretary Mrs. Paula C. Otto, 96 W. Van Ness St., Newburgh, NY 12550
85. CENTRAL OHIO
President Robert H. Gast, 205 Fenway Rd., Columbus, OH 43214
Secretary William L. Hull, 1295 Castleton Rd., Columbus, OH 43220
86. CAPE COD CLOCK WATCHERS
President Barry D. Hutchinson, 14 Chatham Bars Ave., Chatham, MA 02633
Secretary Kenneth H. Goddard, Box 515, 28 Candlewick Ln., W. Hyannis Port, MA 02672
87. GREATER MASSACHUSETTS
President Ms. Linda A. Harris, 45 Pamela Ln., Amesbury, MA 01913
Secretary Burton K. Stineman, 107-H Ethyl Way, Stoughton, MA 02072
88. LONG ISLAND
President Mrs. Rochelle M. Gaenger, 18 School St., E. Williston, NY 11596
Secretary Mervin Levenberg, 166-15 69th Ave., Flushing, NY 11365
89. MAINE
President Capt. J. E. Rehler, USN, Ret., 77 Wentworth St., Portsmouth, NH 03801
Secretary William Gray Eberly, Box 489, R.D. 1, S. Harpswell, ME 04079
90. WESTCHESTER
President Alan Marx, 105 Bayeau Rd., New Rochelle, NY 10804
Secretary
91. HAWKEYE
President Mrs. Erma M. Ruwe, 5413 Aurora #224, Des Moines, IA 50310
Secretary Dr. Joseph Walsh, 8001 Prairie Ave., Urbandale, IA 50322
92. SOUTHWESTERN ONTARIO
President Dr. John Rodney Harle, 711 Algoma Ave., London, Ont., Canada N5X 1W4
Secretary John K. Wood, 684 Galloway Cres., London, Ont., Canada N6J 2Y7
93. SOUTH JERSEY
President Jack Rubin, 1000 Mount Pleasant Way, Cherry Hill, NJ 08034
Secretary Lt. Col. Angelo J. Italiano, 332 Brookline Ave., Cherry Hill, NJ 08002
94. DE ANZA
President Frank F. Specie, 20376 Knollwood Dr., Saratoga, CA 95070
Secretary Robert A. Johnson, 445 N. 15th St., San Jose, CA 95112
95. GOLDEN SPIKE
President George J. Williams, 2337 S. 300 E., Bountiful, UT 84010
Secretary Gary W. Thompson, P.O. Box 1856, Ogden, UT 84402
96. FLORIDA WHITE SANDS
President Paul Jay Geise, 3640 Overland Dr., Pensacola, FL 32504
Secretary Frank A. Bellina, 6135 Virwood Rd., Pensacola, FL 32504
97. GOLDEN EMPIRE
President Ward F. Swank, 1103 N. Stevenson St., Visalia, CA 93291
Secretary Mrs. Gladys Russell, 109 Quincy St., Bakersfield, CA 93305
98. CALOOSA
President Earl Latham, 5574 Buring Ct. SW, Ft. Myers, FL 33907
Secretary Herbert Kilinski, 27252 Gasparillo Dr. SE, Bonita Springs, FL 33923
99. PALM BEACHES OF FLORIDA
President Oscar H. Nelson, 2002 SW 22nd Ave., Boynton Beach, FL 33435
Secretary Leonard W. Rutlin, 5162 Mirror Lakes Blvd., Boynton Beach, FL 33437
100. COLORADO CENTENNIAL
President Mrs. Robert G. Refior, 5543 Saddlerock Trl., Colorado Springs, CO 80918
Secretary Ancel Peckham, 928 Westmoor Dr., Colorado Springs, CO 80904
101. WESTERN MICHIGAN
President Mathew H. Rothert, Jr., 1385 Heather Dr., Holland, MI 49423
Secretary James F. Thornburg, 581 Joy Rd., Battle Creek, MI 49017
102. AMERICAN WATCHMAKERS INSTITUTE
President Orville R. Hagans, 6930 E. Girard Ave., Apt. 408, Denver, CO 80224
Secretary Robert M. Leach, 304 E. University, Urbana, IL 61801
103. ENGLISH
President Allan Wright, P.O. Box 22, Ashford Kent, TN23 1DN England
Secretary Anthony P. Williams, Apple Cottage Ball Ln., Kennington, Ashford Kent, England
104. FIRST QUEENSLAND
President Warren A. Starr, 15 Marginson St., Leichhardt Ipswich, Qld., 4305, Australia
Secretary Peter Tilley, 62 Kertes Rd., Camira, Qld., 4300, Australia
105. THREE RIVERS
President Harry W. Repphan, Jr., 450 Wilson Sq., Evansville, IN 47715
Secretary Robert K. Levi, 1158 Harrelton Ct., Evansville, IN 47715
106. NEW MEXICO ZIA SUNDIALS
President Lt. Col. Donald W. Chance, Sr., 10421 Cielito Lindo NE, Albuquerque, NM 87111
Secretary Homer Newberry, 1408 Cagua Dr. NE, Albuquerque, NM 87110
107. DIABLO VALLEY
President Robert W. Prochnow, P.O. Box 23315, Pleasant Hill, CA 94523
Secretary John S. North, P.O. Box 23315, Pleasant Hill, CA 94523
108. CENTRAL TOKYO
President Shigeru Ono, 5-7-6 Midoricho, Koganeishi, Tokyo, Japan
Secretary Kenichi Ohtsu, 4-23-1-405 Nishi-tsutsujigaoka, Chofu-shi, Tokyo, Japan

109. GREEN MOUNTAIN TIMEKEEPERS SOCIETY
President   Norman J. Boyden, III, Rt. 2-A, 73 Essex Rd., Williston, VT 05495
Secretary   Frederick C. Ringer, Jr., 7 Patricia Pl., Essex Junction, VT 05452
110. RHODE ISLAND
President   Martin D. Saltzman, 24 Maureen Dr., Smithfield, RI 02917
Secretary   Mrs. L. H. Durfee, Escoheag Hill Rd., Escoheag, RI 02821
111. OTTAWA VALLEY
President   William M. Graham, 2-174 Dufferin Rd., Ottawa, Ont., Canada K1M 2A6
Secretary   Peter Bomford, 14 Kinnear St., Ottawa, Ont., Canada K1Y 3R4
112. VALLEY OF THE SUN
President   Emmett J. Sullivan, Jr., 8709 E. Holly, Scottsdale, AZ 85257
Secretary   Earl G. Trevett, 310 W. El Caminito Dr., Phoenix, AZ 85021
113. SOUTHERN ARIZONA
President   Jack Kittle, 1616 E. Calle Altivo, Tucson, AZ 85718
Secretary   Mrs. Gretchen K. Bjorklund, 9325 E. Cathy Pl., Tucson, AZ 85710
114. BROOKLYN
President   Dominick J. Clemente, 1937 E. 9th St., Brooklyn, NY 11223
Secretary   Arthur L. Winakor, 2483 W. 16th St., Apt. 14-C, Brooklyn, NY 11214
115. OLD WEST
President   Robert Kolbe, 1301 S. Duluth, Sioux Falls, SD 57105
Secretary   Edward Varilek, Box 55, Kennebec, SD 57544
116. SANTA ANITA
President   Dr. Howard "Hap" Holladay, 808 Old Mill Rd., San Marino, CA 91108
Secretary   Guadalupe Limon, 4217 Collis Ave., Los Angeles, CA 90032
117. RIO GRANDE
President   Chas. E. Gates, III, P.O. Box 1219, Canutillo, TX 79835
Secretary   Edgar D. Surface, 8408 Cielo Vista, El Paso, TX 79925
118. SAN JOAQUIN VALLEY
President   Paul J. Cauwels, 2891 Dunn Rd., Merced, CA 95340
Secretary   Miss Marie Godbout, 46734 N. Eastwood Dr., Oakhurst, CA 93644
119. QUINTE TIMEKEEPERS
President   Paul W. Kingston, P.O. Box 45, Tweed, Ont., Canada K0K 3J0
Secretary   W. R. Topham, G.B. 7 R.R. 7, Brighton, Ont., Canada K0K 1H0
120. HOROLOGICAL ART
President   Mrs. Rochelle B. Gaenger, 18 School St., E. Williston, NY 11596
Secretary   Mrs. Judy T. Draucker, 1232 Bell Creek Rd., Mechanicsville, VA 23111
121. BRITISH COLUMBIA
President   Dr. I. G. M. Cleator, 1051 Laurier Ave., Vancouver, BC, Canada V6Z 1Y6
Secretary   Ronald D'Altroy, 1007-555 W. 28th St., N. Vancouver, BC, Canada V7N 2J7
122. MELBOURNE
President   Timothy Paul Wilmot, P.O. Box 503, Cheltenham, 3192, Australia
Secretary   John A. McMichael, 1 Worcester St., Huntingdale, Vic., 3166, Australia
123. PRESCOTT HIGH TIMERS
President   John W. Carlson, 659 Navahopi Rd., Sedona, AZ 86336
Secretary   Robert L. Macomber, 639 W. Gurley St., Prescott, AZ 86301
124. LONE STAR
President   Robert M. Wingate, 3237 Dartmoor Ct., Dallas, TX 75229
Secretary   Joe W. Russell, P.O. Box 226030, Dallas, TX 75266
125. MIDWEST ELECTRIC HOROLOGY GROUP
President   Elmer G. Crum, 8510 Harms Rd., Skokie, IL 60077
Secretary   Mrs. Judith Z. Rubin, 3022 W. Jarlath St., Chicago, IL 60645
126. WESTERN CAROLINAS
President   Philip R. Gilbert, 106 Atwood Dr., Hendersonville, NC 28739
Secretary   Mrs. Dorothy D. Gilbert, 106 Atwood, Dr., Hendersonville, NC 28739
127. HEART OF THE NORTH
President   John H. Kirk, 234 E. Monroe Ave., Barron, WI 54812
Secretary   Thomas O. Torgrimson, 2913 Solem Ln., Eau Claire, WI 54701
128. PELICAN STATE
President   Houston C. Jenks, 12265 Parkwood Ave., Baton Rouge, LA 70815
Secretary   Mrs. Charolette S. Carrier, 5767 Hyacinth Ave., Baton Rouge, LA 70808
129. SUNDIAL
President   Eugene T. Hammer, Jr., 719 Clark Dr., Ft. Walton Beach, FL 32548
Secretary   Mrs. Peggy Maselowitch, 564 Hickory Ave., Niceville, FL 32578
130. SUN CITY CLOCK CLUB
President   Lloyd E. Burger, 27050 Howard St., Sun City, CA 92381
Secretary   Mrs. Clara Bevilacqua, 28715 Bradley Rd., Sun City, CA 92381

SEE YOU AT THE
NAWCC COUNCIL SEMINAR
OCTOBER 25-27, 1984 — HARTFORD, CT